AF488188

DESIGNED WITH PURPOSE:
THIS DEVOTIONAL BELONGS TO:

Beloved Daughter of The King

PLUMBED FOR PURPOSE
A Devotional for Spiritual Fruitfulness

Published by TBG Studio Press
Tulsa, Oklahoma

ISBN: 979-8-9944345-3-6

The author and publisher have made every effort to ensure
that the information in this book is accurate at the time of
publication. This devotional is intended for spiritual
encouragement and personal reflection. It is not a substitute
for professional medical, mental health, legal, or pastoral
counsel. Readers are encouraged to seek qualified guidance
for matters requiring such care.

First Edition: 2026

Printed in the United States of America

DEDICATION

To the One who met me in the quiet —
Holy Spirit, thank You for being my guide, my comfort,
and the breath behind these pages. May every woman
who opens this book sense Your nearness.

To Clay —
Thank you for supporting me when the path wasn't
clear. Your quiet faith gave me the space and courage
to keep going.

To my daughters —
You are my answered prayers. May your lives always
be aligned with His Word. This is for you.
All glory to God.

-Michel Hernandez

TABLE OF CONTENTS

INTRODUCTION

THE FRUIT OF ALIGNMENT

I am truly excited for the journey that lies ahead. You have made a wonderful decision. Taking the time to invest in yourself and deepen your understanding of who you are—and *whose* you are—is a choice that, as children of God, we can always cherish. My hope is that you will come to recognize your immense power, grounded in who God is and all the blessings He has in store for you.

As we explore this journey together, let's draw inspiration from the imagery of a plum—a fruit that embodies sweetness, nourishment, and growth. Just as a plum tree flourishes when deeply rooted in rich soil, we, too, can thrive when we align our lives with God's truth. Central to this growth is the concept of the "plumb line," a powerful metaphor in Scripture for measuring and examining our alignment with God's standards.

In Amos 7:7-8, God tells the prophet Amos, "Look, I am setting a plumb line among my people Israel." This imagery invites us to examine our lives and ensure we are growing in a direction that reflects His will. Just as a builder uses a plumb line for stability, we can trust God's Word to guide us toward a fruitful and purposeful life.

This alignment has drawn me closer to God, rooted me deeply in my beliefs, and granted me the freedom to assist others in experiencing the same transformative journey. Together, let's embark on this path, cultivating a life that reflects His divine truth and sweetness!

Remember: You are loved, you are known, and you are seen!

INSTRUCTION PAGE

Use this guide to connect with God each day.

5-Day Structure

This devotional is designed for five days of engagement, leaving you two days for reflection and deeper study. Use these two days to:
Meditate on what God has been teaching you;
Strengthen your understanding.

Set the Scene

Find a Quiet Spot
Choose a calm, distraction-free environment.
Prepare Your Mind
Take a moment to clear your thoughts and welcome God's presence.

But before we dive in!

I want to say this from my heart: I don't know where you are in your journey with God. Maybe you've walked with Jesus for years — or maybe you're not even sure if you've truly given Him your heart.
If that's you, pause here. This could be your moment.
Jesus, I don't have it all figured out, but I know I need You. I open my heart to You now — all of it. Come into my life, lead me, and align me with Your truth. From this day forward, I want to walk with You. Amen.
Whether this is your first yes or your hundredth, welcome. Let's begin — heart open, spirit ready.

START AT THE BEGINNING

Years ago, I had an encounter with the Holy Spirit that profoundly changed the way I understood prayer and my relationship with God. I was deep in sleep when, suddenly, I became fully awake—yet still in a dreamlike state. It was unlike anything I had ever experienced. In that moment, I became aware that I was praying for a man I did not know, led entirely by the Spirit.

As I prayed, I saw myself from a distance, watching as the Holy Spirit resided within me—specifically in my stomach. With each prayer spoken in obedience, the Holy Spirit grew, expanding within me, filling every part of my being. The clearer my prayers became, the stronger God's presence enveloped me.

In that moment of clarity, the Holy Spirit revealed a profound truth: if I did nothing else in life but pray and know God's Word—Jesus, the Living Word—I would fulfill my calling. That revelation has never left me. At first, I thought "knowing the Word" meant mastering Scripture. But I came to understand it was something deeper— knowing Jesus intimately. In Hebrew, the word *yada* means to know someone personally and deeply. This is the kind of relationship God invites us into, and it begins with prayer.

I share this because I know what it feels like to search for direction, to feel lost or uncertain. If that's where you are, I encourage you to start with prayer. Get to know the One who knows you completely. We often complicate life, yet God has made the way clear: talk to Him, seek Jesus in His Word, and trust His voice. When you do, He will lead you. He will reveal His plan, open doors, and fill you with the peace that comes from knowing you are loved and called by the Creator of the universe.

Begin at the beginning. Pray, and know Him.

Daily Steps
I. Read the Scripture

Read Thoughtfully: Read slowly, focusing on the meaning and context.

II. Reflect & Pray

Reflect: Ask, What is God teaching me? How does this apply to my life?

Journal: Write your thoughts, using the provided journaling pages. Explore areas for deeper study or reflection.

Pray: Follow the "P.C.R." pattern:

Praise: Thank God for who He is and what He has done.

Confess: Admit areas where you need God's help.

Request: Ask for the Holy Spirit's guidance and strength.

III. Apply & Act

Identify One Action: Decide on one practical way to live out the lesson from the day.

IV. End with Thanks

Close with Gratitude: Thank God for speaking to you and ask for His wisdom to carry you through the day.

Assessment

Before you begin, take time to complete the <u>Spiritual Growth Assessment</u>. It will help you honestly evaluate where you are spiritually. Return to this assessment at the end of the devotional to reflect on how you've grown and where God is still working in you.

Make It Your Own

Adjust this guide to fit your schedule and spiritual rhythms. Let your time with God bring you peace, clarity, and inspiration!

SPIRITUAL GROWTH

ASSESSMENT

"FROM WITHERING TO FLOURISHING: WHERE ARE YOU?"

UNDERSTANDING LEAVES & ROOTS

Take a moment to reflect on your life—your actions and the deeper beliefs that shape them. The "leaves" represent your outward behaviors, while the "roots" are the beliefs that drive them. Just like a plant's leaves depend on healthy roots, your beliefs shape your actions, and if your roots are unhealthy, your life won't bear the fruit you desire. This assessment will help you explore both the roots and leaves of your life and realign them where needed.

THE PLUMB LINE OF GOD'S TRUTH (AMOS 7:7-8)

In Amos 7:7-8, God uses a plumb line to measure and align His people to His standard of righteousness. The plumb line ensures that structures are straight and aligned. In the same way, God's truth is the measure by which our lives—our beliefs and behaviors—are aligned. Without it, we become crooked and unstable, like a plant leaning out of alignment due to poor roots.

ALIGNING WITH GOD'S TRUTH

This process is about measuring your life against God's plumb line: His Word. As you identify your behaviors and beliefs, ask yourself if they are aligned with His truth. Is your life rooted in God's Word, or are you drawing from unhealthy beliefs that distort your actions?

HEALING & TRANSFORMATION

God desires to transform us from the inside out, aligning our beliefs and behaviors with His will. This assessment is not about condemnation, but about healing and freedom. Let God reveal the roots of your behaviors and help you align them with His purpose. When you live rooted in God's truth, your life will grow strong and bear lasting fruit.

FLOURISHING VOCABULARY GUIDE

Use the following words as inspiration when filling in your plant reflection. These are not just words—they're reflections of your spiritual life and your journey with God.

ROOTS (FOUNDATIONS OF FAITH):

Scripture · Trust · Faith · Identity in Christ · Truth · Stability · Obedience · Fellowship · Surrender · Hope · Discipline · Humility · Devotion · Dependence · Integrity

LEAVES (VISIBLE FRUIT & GROWTH):

Joy · Peace · Patience · Kindness · Self-Control · Compassion · Boldness · Forgiveness · Wisdom · Generosity · Gentleness · Discernment · Gratitude · Love · Worship

WATERING CAN (NOURISHMENT SOURCES):

Prayer · Worship · God's Word · Community · Silence & Solitude · Teaching · Rest · Repentance · Encouragement · Gratitude · Fasting · Journaling · Presence of God · Accountability · Holy Spirit

FLOURISHING

Withering Vocabulary Guide

Use the following words as a guide to reflect on areas of spiritual disconnection or struggle. These words are not to bring shame, but to bring awareness and an invitation to let God begin a new work of renewal in you.

ROOTS (Unhealthy or Unstable Foundations):

Doubt · Fear · Distraction · Busyness · Pride · Shame · Insecurity · Isolation · Bitterness · Control · Worry · Unbelief · Unforgiveness · Comparison · Rebellion

LEAVES (Visible Struggles or Signs of Withering):

Anxiety · Anger · Apathy · Impatience · Frustration · Jealousy · Disconnection · Resentment · Exhaustion · Spiritual Numbness · Hopelessness · Critical Spirit · Burnout · Disobedience · Self-Reliance

WATERING CAN (Toxic or Lacking Sources of Nourishment):

Neglect · Social Media Overload · People-Pleasing · Constant Noise · Negative Influences Isolation · Self-Doubt · Bitterness · Worldly Distractions · Unconfessed Sin · Emotional · Exhaustion · Overcommitment · Lack of Prayer · Surface-Level Faith · Fear of Vulnerability

Use this list to help you name the areas God is inviting you to uproot, prune, or refresh. Healing and growth begin with honesty, and God meets you there.

WITHERING

SELFISHNESS
IGNORANCE
RESTLESNESS
SPIRITUAL
NEGLECT
ISOLATION
anxiety
anger
jealousy
apathy
burnout
numbness
self-
reliance
disconnection
critical
spirit
bitterness
busyness
insecurity
unbelief
comparison
pride
doubt
unforgiveness

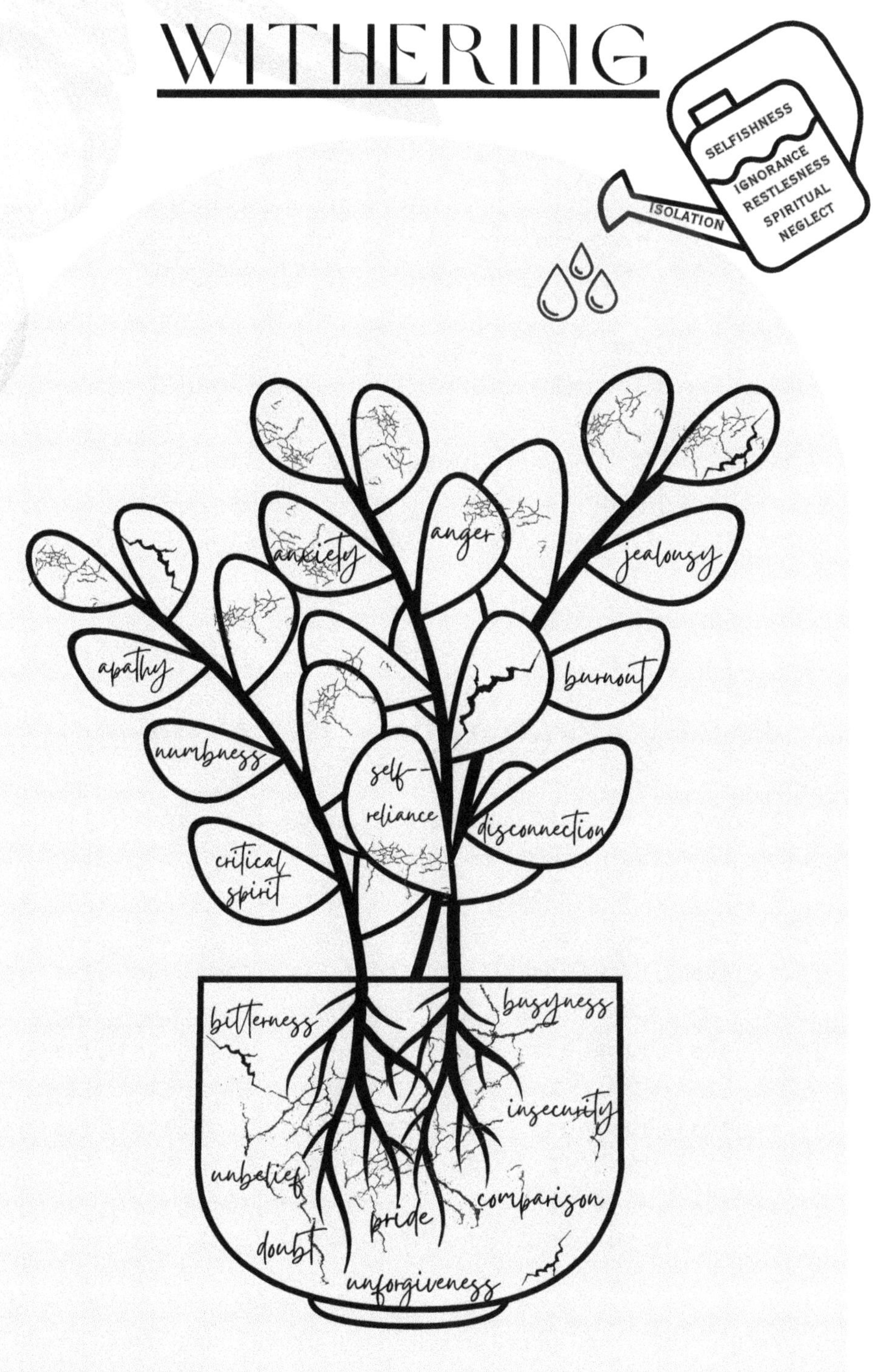

Spiritual Growth Assessment

Visualizing Your Spiritual Growth

Look at the image of the potted *plants on pages 14 and 15*. This illustration represents our spiritual life:

A Flourishing Plant – Deep roots, vibrant leaves, and steady nourishment. This reflects a heart strengthened by God's Word and presence.
A Withering Plant – Weak roots, drooping leaves, and dry soil. This represents spiritual disconnection and neglect.

PART 1: Approaching the Assessment

1. Find a quiet space to reflect.
2. Pray and invite the Holy Spirit to reveal your spiritual state.
3. Answer honestly — awareness is the first step to growth.
4. Use your reflections to take steps toward spiritual renewal.

Reflection Questions (Use the Journaling Pages)
- Are my spiritual roots deep and grounded in God's Word?
- Do I regularly seek God's presence for nourishment?
- Is there evidence of spiritual fruit in my life?
- Am I allowing God to prune areas that hinder growth?
- What does my spiritual environment look like?
- What areas feel healthy, and what areas feel stagnant?
- How can I better align myself with God's purpose?

Date

YOU WERE NOT CREATED BY ACCIDENT, BUT DESIGNED
WITH DIVINE PRECISION FOR A PURPOSE ONLY YOU CAN FULFILL.

SPIRITUAL GROWTH ASSESSMENT

PART 2: PERSONAL REFLECTION ACTIVITY

Using the blank plant image provided, create a visual representation of your spiritual condition:

ROOTS – WHAT FORMS YOUR FOUNDATION? ARE YOU DEEPLY ROOTED IN FAITH, OR DO YOUR ROOTS FEEL WEAK?

LEAVES – WHAT IS VISIBLE IN YOUR SPIRITUAL LIFE? ARE YOU BEARING FRUIT, OR DO YOU SEE SIGNS OF STRUGGLE?

WATERING CAN – WHAT ARE YOU FEEDING YOUR SPIRIT? ARE YOU CONSISTENTLY NOURISHED, OR DO YOU FEEL SPIRITUALLY DEHYDRATED?

Fill in your plant with words that represent your current spiritual state. You can reference the vocabulary word sheets provided or add your own. There are no wrong answers. No matter where you are, growth is always possible. God, the ultimate Gardener, desires to nourish and strengthen you so that you may flourish in His purpose.

WHERE I AM

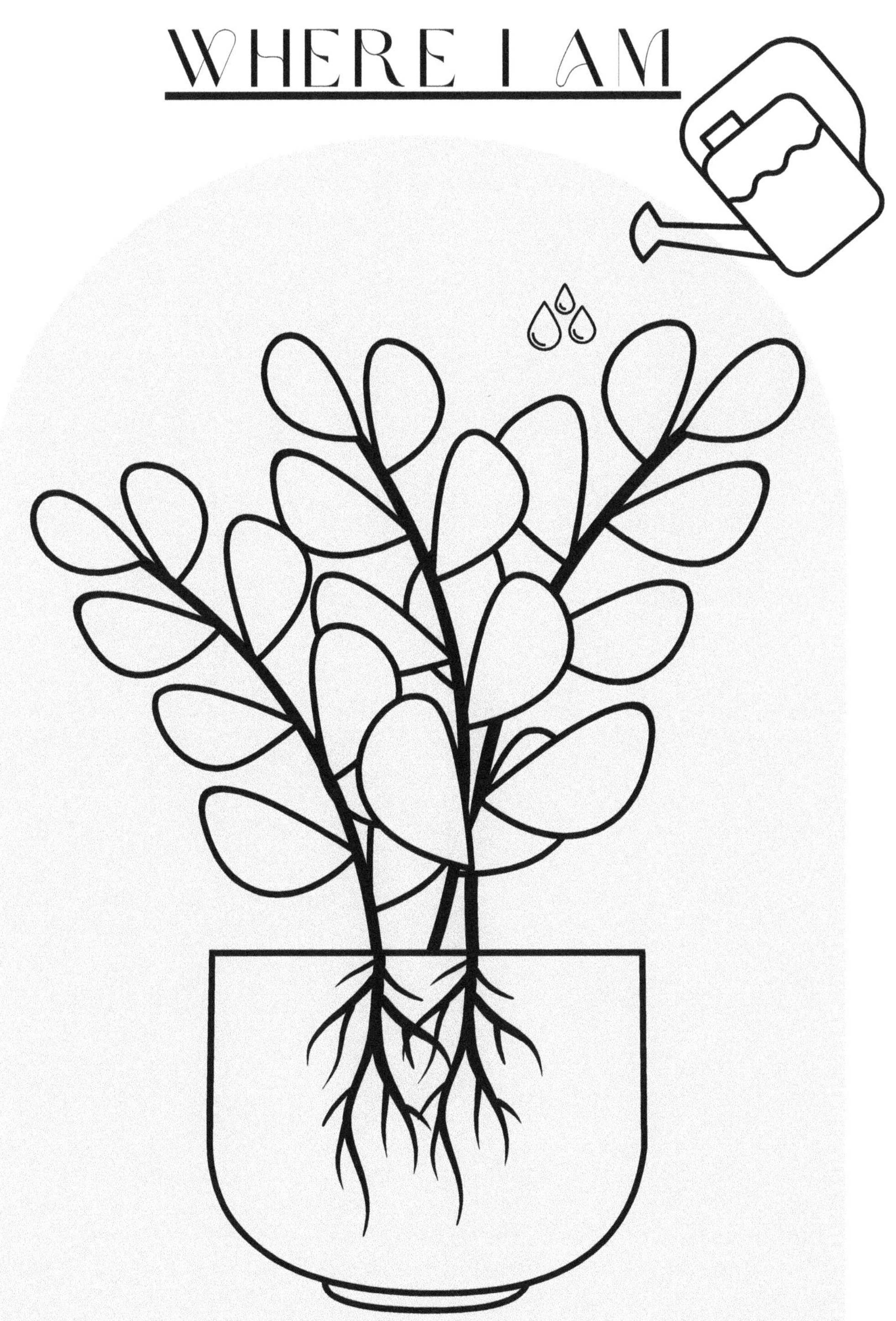

ROOTED
IN CHRIST

Purpose Revealed

An Invitation to Go Deeper: Rooted in Christ

In the early days of my faith journey, I experienced a vision that profoundly shaped my understanding of being rooted in Christ. In this vision, I stood within a towering structure made of massive stones, bridging the realms of earth and heaven. The air around me was saturated with the unmistakable presence of holiness.
To my left, an enormous window revealed a serene display of drifting clouds, bathed in radiant, warm, and welcoming light. Directly in front of me stood Jesus. His gaze was captivating—His eyes shimmering with an indescribable brilliance, as though they contained the essence of the universe itself. They were like deep wells with no end, drawing me in with both awe and peace.

His golden hair glowed with a light that radiated from within— undeniably the presence of the Holy Spirit, alive and overflowing. It wasn't just light; it was life, and I could feel it. His robe of royal blue flowed with an elegance that spoke of His majesty and grace. I couldn't help but think to myself how soft it must feel.

As I stood in awe, taking in what I was seeing, I noticed Jesus with both of His arms extended to His left, as if inviting me toward a stationary escalator suspended in the air. This escalator led directly to heaven, where streams of light poured out from behind what looked like a thin veil. Shadows of people moved with purpose, walking toward a set destination.
To my right, I saw a bustling highway of angels, each carrying a unique message—representing distinct pieces of heavenly communication. I had a deep knowing that these angels were on their way to specific individuals on earth.

Initially, I understood the vision as an invitation to salvation. But as I continued to meditate on it, a deeper meaning began to unfold. Jesus wasn't merely reminding me of salvation—He was inviting me into a more intimate and transformative relationship with Him. Salvation is the foundation, but being rooted in Christ calls us to move beyond that starting point and choose to grow in faith each day.

The stationary escalator in the vision symbolized the gift of free will. It reminded me that while the way to heaven has been made accessible through Christ, we are called to actively engage in the journey of faith.

Each day, we must take deliberate steps to grow deeper in our relationship with Him, drawing nourishment from God's Word, surrendering our struggles, and allowing His Spirit to transform us.

Like the challenge presented in the book Not a Fan by Kyle Idleman, we're invited to move beyond mere admiration of Jesus and become committed followers.This means abiding in Him, trusting His lead, and allowing His truth to shape our thoughts and actions.

Let this vision serve as a reminder that salvation is not the end, but the beginning of a lifelong journey. God desires for us to experience the fullness of His love and presence, to be rooted deeply in Him. When we respond to His daily invitations, we step closer to our true selves—individuals created to shine brightly for His glory.

May we each choose, moment by moment, to draw near to Jesus, allowing our faith to deepen and our lives to reflect the beauty of His presence.

DAY I

ROOTED IN CHRIST

Scripture Reading: 2 Corinthians 5:17 (NIV)

OUR IDENTITY IN CHRIST
"Therefore, if anyone is in Christ, the new creation has come:
The old has gone, the new is here!"

REFLECTION:
Our identity is often shaped by past experiences,
achievements, and relationships. But in Christ, our identity is
made new. We are no longer defined by what we've done or
what's been done to us—we are defined by His grace.

PRAYER:
Lord, thank You for making me a new creation in Christ. Help
me to fully embrace my identity in You and to let go of the
things that do not align with who You say I am. Amen.

CONTEMPLATION:
What old labels or beliefs are holding you back? Write them
down. Surrender them to God, and invite Him to redefine you
through His Word.

Aligning Your Thoughts

YOU WERE NOT CREATED BY ACCIDENT, BUT DESIGNED
WITH DIVINE PRECISION FOR A PURPOSE ONLY YOU CAN FULFILL.

DAY II

ROOTED IN CHRIST

Scripture Reading: John 8:32 (NIV)

ROOTED IN GOD'S TRUTH

"Then you will know the truth, and the truth will set you free."

REFLECTION:

Scripture reveals the truth about who God is and who we are in Him. Understanding and internalizing these truths is essential for living a life of freedom and purpose. God's Word is not just a book but a guide that shapes our thoughts, actions, and identity. As we delve into Scripture, we uncover more about our identity and His promises.

PRAYER:

Heavenly Father, guide me as I study Your Word. Help me to understand and live out the truths revealed in Scripture. May Your truth set me free from any lies or misconceptions. Amen.

CONTEMPLATION:

Spend some time reading a passage of Scripture that speaks to your identity in Christ. Reflect on how this truth applies to your life, and jot down any insights or changes you feel called to make.

Date ________________

____
____
____
____
____
____
____
____
____
____
____
____
____
____

YOU WERE NOT CREATED BY ACCIDENT, BUT DESIGNED
WITH DIVINE PRECISION FOR A PURPOSE ONLY YOU CAN FULFILL.

DAY III

ROOTED IN CHRIST

Scripture Reading: Galatians 2:20 (NIV)

LIVING OUT OUR IDENTITY

"I have been crucified with Christ and I no longer live, but Christ lives in me. The life I now live in the body, I live by faith in the Son of God, who loved me and gave himself for me."

REFLECTION:

Our identity in Christ is not just a belief but a way of life. When we accept Jesus, our lives are intertwined with His. This means our actions, thoughts, and decisions should reflect His love and grace. Living out our identity involves embodying Christ's character in every aspect of our lives.

PRAYER:

Lord Jesus, help me to live out my identity in You each day. Let my actions reflect Your love and grace, and guide me to live by faith in every situation. Amen.

CONTEMPLATION:

Think about a specific area of your life where you find it challenging to live out your identity in Christ. Ask God for strength and guidance to align this area with His will.

YOU WERE NOT CREATED BY ACCIDENT, BUT DESIGNED
WITH DIVINE PRECISION FOR A PURPOSE ONLY YOU CAN FULFILL.

DAY IV

ROOTED IN CHRIST

Scripture Reading: 1 Peter 2:9 (NIV)

EMBRACING OUR ROLE IN THE FAMILY OF GOD
"But you are a chosen people, a royal priesthood, a holy nation, God's special possession, that you may declare the praises of him who called you out of darkness into his wonderful light."

REFLECTION:
As members of God's family, we have a significant role and purpose. We are chosen, set apart, and called to declare His praises. This role is not only about personal transformation but also about contributing to the broader mission of spreading God's light and love to the world.

PRAYER:
Father, thank You for choosing me and making me part of Your royal priesthood. Help me to embrace my role in Your family and to live in a way that declares Your praises to others. Amen.

CONTEMPLATION:
Consider how you can contribute to the mission of God's family in your community. Write down one practical step you can take to fulfill your role and make a difference.

Aligning Your Thoughts

Date
____

YOU WERE NOT CREATED BY ACCIDENT, BUT DESIGNED
WITH DIVINE PRECISION FOR A PURPOSE ONLY YOU CAN FULFILL.

DAY V

ROOTED IN CHRIST

Scripture Reading: Philippians 4:13 (NIV)

STRENGTHENED BY CHRIST
"I can do all this through him who gives me strength."

REFLECTION:
Our strength and capability come from Christ. No matter what challenges we face or how inadequate we might feel, we can rely on Christ's strength to see us through. Our identity in Him equips us with power and confidence to face life's difficulties and to live out our purpose.

PRAYER:
Lord, I acknowledge that my strength comes from You. In moments of weakness or struggle, remind me of Your power working in and through me. Help me to trust in Your strength and rely on You completely. Amen.

CONTEMPLATION:
Reflect on a recent challenge or difficulty.
Write a prayer asking for Christ's strength in that situation, and trust Him to provide the power you need.

Date

YOU WERE NOT CREATED BY ACCIDENT, BUT DESIGNED
WITH DIVINE PRECISION FOR A PURPOSE ONLY YOU CAN FULFILL.

Identity Before Assignment

THIS IS PLUMB 

I am who God says I am — before I do anything for Him.

THIS IS NOT 

My value comes from what I accomplish.

*"Before I formed you in the womb
I knew you..." – Jeremiah 1:5*

CLOSING JOURNAL:

ROOTED IN CHRIST

LOOKING AHEAD
What step can I take next week to stay firmly rooted in Christ?
This prompt encourages meaningful reflection while fostering
gratitude, prayer,
and intentionality for the week ahead.

1. REFLECTION ON THE WEEK
What moments this week made me feel deeply connected to Christ?
Were there any challenges that tested my spiritual foundation? How
did I respond?

2. GROWTH AND INSIGHTS
What has God revealed to me about being rooted in Him?
How has my understanding of His Word shaped my thoughts or
actions this week?

3. GRATITUDE
List three specific ways I experienced God's presence or faithfulness
this week.

4. PRAYER OF COMMITMENT
Write a prayer asking God to deepen your roots in Him,
acknowledging areas
where you need strength or growth.

Aligning Your Thoughts

Date

YOU WERE NOT CREATED BY ACCIDENT, BUT DESIGNED
WITH DIVINE PRECISION FOR A PURPOSE ONLY YOU CAN FULFILL.

DOMINION
&
AUTHORITY

PURPOSE REVEALED

AUTHORITY AND DOMINION: RISING ABOVE THE FOG

As I've grown in my faith, God has used dreams to mirror my spiritual journey—vivid reflections of struggles and triumphs that illuminate the truth of who I am in Christ. One dream, in particular, revealed the authority we carry as followers of Jesus.

In the dream, I was driving at night toward a destination I knew was undeniably ordained by God.
The road ahead was busy with traffic going in both directions and lined with traffic lights, yet my heart pulsed with purpose and determination.
Suddenly, a thick fog enveloped my car, obscuring my view and leaving me disoriented.
It was a stark reflection of those moments in life when doubt and confusion cloud our vision.

As I struggled to regain clarity and make sense of what was happening, my attention shifted to a menacing presence behind me—a demon, sinister and intent on impeding my progress. Fear gripped my heart as its oppressive energy filled the space around me. But in the midst of my panic, I remembered the truths I had learned: I am a child of God, filled with the Spirit, and equipped with divine authority.

Summoning courage, I let go of the steering wheel and turned to face the darkness head-on. With unwavering conviction, I declared my identity in Christ and rebuked the demon in the name of Jesus. As the words left my mouth, the demon's aggression faded—it became passive, its power diminished. This victory was a powerful reminder of the dominion we possess as believers to confront and overcome spiritual adversity.

PURPOSE REVEALED

The authority we carry as followers of Christ is not our own—it is rooted in Him. In Luke 10:19, Jesus says, "I have given you authority to trample on snakes and scorpions and to overcome all the power of the enemy; nothing will harm you." This promise equips us to stand firm against fear, doubt, and spiritual attack.

My dream illustrated this truth in a tangible way: the fog symbolized the obstacles that obscure our path, and the demon represented the spiritual forces that seek to derail us. Yet, as believers, we are empowered by the Spirit to rise above the fog and confront the darkness, armed with the truth of our faith.

This authority isn't just for moments of spiritual warfare. It's a daily reality that allows us to walk in confidence and clarity. Life's challenges may attempt to overwhelm us, but when we embrace our identity in Christ, we can navigate even the darkest roads with peace, knowing we are not alone.

I share this experience as an encouragement. You, too, have been given authority through Christ. Whether you're facing spiritual battles, doubts, or fears, remember that you are equipped to overcome. Lean into your faith, speak truth over your circumstances, and walk forward with boldness. As you do, you'll not only find clarity for your own journey but will also illuminate the way for others, reminding them of the strength and dominion we all carry as children of God.

DAY I

DOMINION & AUTHORITY

Scripture Reading: Romans 6:6-14 (NIV)

AUTHORITY OVER SIN

"For we know that our old self was crucified with him so that the body ruled by sin might be done away with, that we should no longer be slaves to sin—because anyone who has died has been set free from sin... Therefore do not let sin reign in your mortal body so that you obey its evil desires."

REFLECTION:

Through Jesus' death and resurrection, we have been given authority over sin. We are no longer slaves to sin but are set free to live in righteousness. Consider areas in your life where sin still feels powerful and how Christ's victory enables you to overcome. His strength is sufficient to break the chains and empower you to live in freedom.

PRAYER:

Lord Jesus, thank You for Your sacrifice that sets me free from the power of sin. Help me to remember I am no longer a slave to my old ways but a new creation in You. Strengthen me to resist temptation and guide me to walk in Your righteousness. Amen.

CONTEMPLATION:

Identify one area in your life where you struggle with sin. Write a prayer asking for Christ's power to overcome it. Commit to a daily practice of prayer or seek accountability to help you grow in freedom and holiness.

Date
....

YOU WERE NOT CREATED BY ACCIDENT, BUT DESIGNED
WITH DIVINE PRECISION FOR A PURPOSE ONLY YOU CAN FULFILL.

DAY II

DOMINION & AUTHORITY

Scripture Reading: John 14:13-14 (NIV); Hebrews 4:16 (NIV)

AUTHORITY IN PRAYER
"And I will do whatever you ask in my name, so that the Father may be glorified in the Son. You may ask me for anything in my name, and I will do it."
"Let us then approach God's throne of grace with confidence, so that we may receive mercy and find grace to help us in our time of need."

REFLECTION:
Through Christ, we are granted the incredible privilege of approaching God's throne of grace with confidence. We are given authority to ask in Jesus' name, trusting that God will answer according to His will. Reflect on how this access to God impacts your prayer life and your intimacy with Him. Know that you are heard and that your prayers align with God's greater purposes.

PRAYER:
Heavenly Father, thank You for the authority You've given me to approach You boldly in prayer. Thank You for the access I have through Jesus. Help me to pray with faith and trust, aligning my heart with Your will. Guide my prayers to bring glory to You. Amen.

CONTEMPLATION:
Take a moment to reflect on a specific prayer request. Write a prayer asking for God's will to be done in that situation, trusting that He will hear and answer according to His purpose. Pray boldly in Jesus' name, knowing that God is at work.

Date

DAY III

DOMINION & AUTHORITY

Scripture Reading: Luke 10:19 (NIV); Ephesians 6:12 (NIV)

AUTHORITY OVER SPIRITUAL FORCES

"I have given you authority to trample on snakes and scorpions, and to overcome all the power of the enemy; nothing will harm you."

"For our struggle is not against flesh and blood, but against the rulers, against the authorities, against the powers of this dark world and against the spiritual forces of evil in the heavenly realms."

REFLECTION:

Jesus has granted us authority to overcome all spiritual forces of darkness. Our struggle is not merely against physical challenges but against spiritual forces that seek to deceive, oppress, and lead us astray. Reflect on how this authority allows you to stand firm in the face of spiritual attacks and claim victory in Christ. Consider any areas of your life where you sense spiritual opposition and how you can confront them with His power.

PRAYER:

Lord, thank You for giving me the authority to stand firm against the spiritual forces of darkness. Strengthen me to resist the enemy and to walk in the victory You have secured for me. Help me to be discerning in spiritual matters and to trust in Your protection. Amen.

CONTEMPLATION:

Identify an area of your life where you feel spiritual attack or oppression. Write a prayer, using Scripture, to stand firm against the enemy and claim the authority Jesus has given you. Pray in the powerful name of Jesus for protection and victory.

Aligning Your Thoughts

Date

YOU WERE NOT CREATED BY ACCIDENT, BUT DESIGNED
WITH DIVINE PRECISION FOR A PURPOSE ONLY YOU CAN FULFILL.

DAY IV

DOMINION & AUTHORITY

Scripture Reading: Matthew 28:18-20 (NIV)

AUTHORITY TO SHARE THE GOSPEL

"Then Jesus came to them and said, 'All authority in heaven and on earth has been given to me. Therefore go and make disciples of all nations, baptizing them in the name of the Father and of the Son and of the Holy Spirit, and teaching them to obey everything I have commanded you. And surely I am with you always, to the very end of the age.'"

REFLECTION:

Jesus has entrusted us with the authority to share the gospel and make disciples of all nations. This calling is not just for the apostles but for all believers. Reflect on your role in fulfilling the Great Commission.
Consider how you can actively proclaim the good news and lead others
to Christ, whether in your daily conversations or through intentional evangelistic efforts.

PRAYER:

Lord, thank You for the authority You've given me to share the gospel and make disciples. Give me boldness to speak Your truth and compassion to reach those who don't yet know You. Guide me in fulfilling this Great Commission, and help me be faithful in my witness. Amen.

CONTEMPLATION:

Reach out to someone in your life who may need to hear the gospel. Write a prayer asking God to provide opportunities for you to share His message of salvation. Consider how you can support evangelistic efforts or missions in your community or beyond.

Aligning Your Thoughts

Date __________________

YOU WERE NOT CREATED BY ACCIDENT, BUT DESIGNED
WITH DIVINE PRECISION FOR A PURPOSE ONLY YOU CAN FULFILL.

DAY V

DOMINION & AUTHORITY

Scripture Reading: Mark 16:17-18 (NIV); Luke 9:1-2 (NIV)

AUTHORITY TO HEAL AND RESTORE

"And these signs will accompany those who believe: In my name they will drive out demons; they will speak in new tongues; they will pick up snakes with their hands; and when they drink deadly poison, it will not hurt them at all; they will place their hands on sick people, and they will get well."

"When Jesus had called the Twelve together, he gave them power and authority to drive out all demons and to cure diseases, and he sent them out to proclaim the kingdom of God and to heal the sick."

REFLECTION:

Jesus has given us the authority to heal and restore in His name. Reflect on the power we have to pray for healing and to minister restoration to those in need. Consider how you can be a vessel for God's healing, whether through prayer, compassion, or practical support. Recognize that you are called to be an instrument of His love and restoration in a broken world.

PRAYER:

Lord, thank You for the authority You've given me to pray for healing and to bring restoration through Your name. Fill me with faith and compassion as I seek to minister to those in need. Guide me in using this authority to bring Your kingdom to earth and to restore lives in Your power. Amen.

CONTEMPLATION:

Look for someone in your life who needs prayer or healing. Write a prayer asking God to guide you in offering support, healing, and encouragement. Commit to praying for them and finding practical ways to help.

YOU WERE NOT CREATED BY ACCIDENT, BUT DESIGNED
WITH DIVINE PRECISION FOR A PURPOSE ONLY YOU CAN FULFILL.

PURPOSE IS REVEALED IN SURRENDER

THIS IS PLUMB

Purpose unfolds when I release control.

THIS IS NOT

I have to hustle to find my calling.

"In all your ways submit to Him, and He will make your paths straight." – Proverbs 3:6

CLOSING JOURNAL:

DOMINION & AUTHORITY

THIS PROMPT EMPHASIZES REFLECTION, GRATITUDE, AND ACTIONABLE FAITH, ALIGNING WITH THE THEME OF LIVING BOLDLY IN GOD'S AUTHORITY.

1. REFLECTION ON THE WEEK

How did I walk in the authority God has given me this week?
Were there moments where I hesitated to step into the dominion I've been
called to? Why?

2. LESSONS AND INSIGHTS

What has God taught me about my identity and authority in Christ?
How did I see His power working through me or around me?

3. VICTORY AND CHALLENGES

What victories did I experience as I exercised dominion in my life?
What challenges showed me areas where I need to grow in faith or confidence
in God's power?

4. GRATITUDE

List three ways God's authority and sovereignty were evident in my
life this week.

5. PRAYER OF ALIGNMENT

Write a prayer declaring your trust in God's authority and committing to walk
boldly in His dominion next week.

6. INTENTIONAL NEXT STEPS

What specific area of my life do I need to submit to God's authority
or exercise my God-given dominion over in the coming week?

Date

YOU WERE NOT CREATED BY ACCIDENT, BUT DESIGNED
WITH DIVINE PRECISION FOR A PURPOSE ONLY YOU CAN FULFILL.

PRAYER. RENEWAL. DECLARATION.

MOVING FROM ROUTINE TO RELEASE

Purpose Revealed

The Power of Prayer: Releasing the Butterflies

One night, I had a dream that further shaped my understanding of prayer. I found myself in a vast warehouse, lying face down in a posture of surrender. The atmosphere was thick —still and sacred, as if heaven had drawn near. Resting on my back were vibrant, delicate butterflies, each carrying a small scroll wrapped in cellophane. They looked like butterfly lollipops, and I instinctively knew they were not just decorative—they were unspoken prayers yet to be released.

As I lay there, I felt the fire of the Holy Spirit resting on me—a tangible sign of His presence and a quiet commissioning for the intercessory work to come.

Around me stood shelves filled with more of these butterflies—prayers not born from personal longing, but divinely appointed moments of intercession, waiting to be released in alignment with God's will.

As I slowly stood, the butterflies rose with me. A presence beside me— whom I recognized as a friend but knew was an angel—gently assured me that I wasn't alone in this sacred assignment. I understood then: these butterflies symbolized prayers ready to be spoken. Once released, they would rise toward heaven like incense before God's throne (Revelation 5:8). Prayer was no longer just a spiritual discipline—it had become a living, breathing connection to the heart of God.

Each scroll was a divine invitation to partner with heaven—an opportunity to pray "Your kingdom come, Your will be done, on earth as it is in heaven" (Matthew 6:10).

Prayer is both a privilege and a responsibility. It lifts burdens, carries hope, and releases God's will into the world. As we align our hearts with His and pray by the Spirit, our words become messengers that ascend to heaven and accomplish His purpose.

May we release the butterflies of hope and transformation with faith, knowing our prayers will not return empty but will fulfill all that God intends (Isaiah 55:11).

DAY I

PRAYER. RENEWAL. DECLARATION.

Scripture Reading: John 15:3 (NIV)

CLEANSING THROUGH THE WORD
"You are already clean because of the word I have spoken to you."

REFLECTION:
Jesus likens His words to a cleansing agent. As we immerse ourselves in Scripture, we are spiritually washed and purified. The Word of God cleanses us from sin, renews our minds, and helps us to grow in Christ. This daily practice of reading and meditating on the Bible is essential for maintaining our spiritual health and closeness to God.

PRAYER:
Lord, thank You for the cleansing power of Your Word. As I read and meditate on Scripture today, purify my heart and mind. Let Your Word wash over me and transform me to reflect Your image. Amen.

CONTEMPLATION:
Spend some time reading a passage from the Bible. Ask the Holy Spirit to reveal any areas in your life where you need cleansing and to help you apply His Word to those areas.

Aligning Your Thoughts

Date

YOU WERE NOT CREATED BY ACCIDENT, BUT DESIGNED
WITH DIVINE PRECISION FOR A PURPOSE ONLY YOU CAN FULFILL.

DAY II

PRAYER. RENEWAL. DECLARATION.

Scripture Reading: 1 Corinthians 14:2 (NIV)

THE POWER OF PRAYING IN TONGUES

"For anyone who speaks in a tongue does not speak to people but to God. Indeed, no one understands them; they utter mysteries by the Spirit."

REFLECTION:

Praying in tongues is a profound way to connect with God and build your spirit. It allows you to communicate with God beyond your natural understanding and access divine mysteries. This form of prayer can be a powerful tool for personal edification and spiritual growth.

PRAYER:

Holy Spirit, I invite You to lead me in praying in tongues. Help me to yield to Your guidance and experience the depth of communion that comes through this gift. Strengthen my spirit, and draw me closer to You. Amen.

CONTEMPLATION:

If you have the gift of tongues, take some time to pray in the Spirit. If not, ask God to deepen your understanding of this gift and to lead you in other ways of building your spiritual life.

Aligning Your Thoughts

Date

YOU WERE NOT CREATED BY ACCIDENT, BUT DESIGNED
WITH DIVINE PRECISION FOR A PURPOSE ONLY YOU CAN FULFILL.

DAY IV

PRAYER. RENEWAL. DECLARATION.

Scripture Reading: Psalm 119:11 (NIV)

INTEGRATING PRAYER AND THE WORD
"I have hidden your word in my heart that I might not sin against you."

REFLECTION:
Integrating prayer and the Word of God enhances our spiritual life. As we pray, we can meditate on Scripture verses, allowing them to guide and shape our prayers. This practice strengthens our faith and aligns our desires with God's will.

PRAYER:
Father, help me to weave Your Word into my prayers, letting Scripture guide my conversations with You and transform my understanding.
May Your Word be deeply embedded into my heart and influence all aspects of my life. Amen.

CONTEMPLATION:
Choose a Scripture verse to focus on today. As you pray, meditate on this verse and ask God how He wants it to influence your thoughts and actions.

Aligning Your Thoughts

Date

YOU WERE NOT CREATED BY ACCIDENT, BUT DESIGNED
WITH DIVINE PRECISION FOR A PURPOSE ONLY YOU CAN FULFILL.

DAY V

PRAYER. RENEWAL. DECLARATION.

"Finally, be strong in the Lord and in his mighty power."
Scripture Reading: Ephesians 6:10 (NIV)

STRENGTH THROUGH CLEANSING AND DECLARING

REFLECTION:
Our strength and ability to overcome challenges come from being rooted in Christ and applying His Word in our lives. Cleansing through Scripture and decreeing His promises are integral to walking in His strength and power. These practices help us to stand firm and be effective in our spiritual journey.

PRAYER:
Lord, thank You for the strength You provide through Your Word and the power of decreeing Your promises. Help me remain steadfast in You and utilize the tools You've given me to live a victorious life. Amen.

CONTEMPLATION:
Reflect on how the practices of cleansing, praying in tongues, and decreeing have impacted your spiritual journey. Write down any insights or commitments you feel led to make moving forward.

Aligning Your Thoughts

Date

YOU WERE NOT CREATED BY ACCIDENT, BUT DESIGNED
WITH DIVINE PRECISION FOR A PURPOSE ONLY YOU CAN FULFILL.

LEGACY IS BUILT
IN
THE DAILY

THIS IS PLUMB

What I do in secret shapes generations.

THIS IS NOT

My ordinary moments don't matter.

"Well done, good and faithful servant…" – Matthew 25:23

CLOSING JOURNAL:

PRAYER. RENEWAL. DECLARATION.

1. REFLECTION ON PRAYER

How consistent and heartfelt was my prayer life this week?
What prayers did I see answered, and how did they impact my faith?
Were there areas where I struggled to trust God in prayer?

2. SPIRITUAL RENEWAL

What brought refreshment to my spirit this week?
How did God reveal areas in my life needing renewal or
transformation?
In what ways did I sense His presence renewing my strength or
perspective?

3. PROPHETIC DECREES

What truths or promises from God's Word did I declare over my life or
circumstances?
How did speaking God's promises impact my mindset or situation?
What new declarations do I feel led to make moving forward?

4. GRATITUDE AND ACKNOWLEDGMENT

List three ways God showed His faithfulness, power, or renewal this
week.

5. PRAYER FOR ALIGNMENT

Write a prayer aligning your heart with God's will, asking for
continued renewal and boldness to speak His truth over your life.

6. VISION FOR THE WEEK AHEAD

What specific area of my life will I focus on in prayer, seek renewal, or
declare God's promises over next week?

This prompt encourages deep reflection, gratitude, and intentional
preparation for walking in prayer, renewal, and faith-filled decrees.

Date ____________

YOU WERE NOT CREATED BY ACCIDENT, BUT DESIGNED
WITH DIVINE PRECISION FOR A PURPOSE ONLY YOU CAN FULFILL.

FASTING

AS JESUS FASTED

PURPOSE REVEALED

FASTING LIKE JESUS: A LIFESTYLE OF ALIGNMENT

Initially, I didn't understand the concept of fasting. I thought that if I gave up food, it was to get something in return. But as I grew in my relationship with God and learned more about the spiritual depth and power of fasting, everything changed. I began to experience breakthroughs—not just personally, but in my marriage and in the lives of my children. Fasting brought spiritual acceleration that nothing else had.

In our modern culture, food holds a central role in how we socialize, celebrate, and even how we comfort ourselves. But when I began to incorporate fasting as a regular rhythm in my life, it helped me identify where my flesh was taking the lead. It's not always easy. In fact, it's a constant battle. But fasting keeps me spiritually sharp and reminds me of my true source of strength.

If you haven't yet adopted a lifestyle of fasting, I want to encourage you to start. Begin slowly, prayerfully, and with grace. Fasting is more than abstaining from food. It's a spiritual positioning. It aligns your heart and mind with the Father and opens your spirit to hear from Him more clearly. It strips away distractions, quiets the noise, and increases your sensitivity to the Holy Spirit.

Jesus fasted. He modeled for us what it looks like to surrender the physical in pursuit of the spiritual. And when we fast like He did, not for performance, but for purpose, we position ourselves to receive from God in powerful and transformative ways.

Let fasting become a tool for realignment. Let it be a lifestyle of intimacy, breakthrough, and surrender. I promise it will change everything.

DAY I

FASTING AS JESUS FASTED

Scripture Reading: Matthew 4:1-2 (NIV)

THE PURPOSE OF FASTING
"Then Jesus was led by the Spirit into the wilderness to be tempted by the devil. After fasting forty days and forty nights, he was hungry."

REFLECTION:
Fasting is a practice deeply rooted in Scripture, and Jesus Himself fasted as part of His preparation for ministry. It's not just about abstaining from food but about drawing closer to God, seeking His will, and gaining spiritual strength. Jesus fasted to prepare Himself for the trials ahead and to deepen His reliance on God. Similarly, our fasting should be a time of focused spiritual growth and dependence on the Father.

PRAYER:
Lord, as I embark on this journey of fasting, help me to understand its
true purpose. Guide me in drawing nearer to You and seeking Your will above all else. Amen.

CONTEMPLATION:
Reflect on why you are choosing to fast. Write down your motivations and what you hope to discover, spiritually, during this period.

Aligning Your Thoughts

Date ....

YOU WERE NOT CREATED BY ACCIDENT, BUT DESIGNED
WITH DIVINE PRECISION FOR A PURPOSE ONLY YOU CAN FULFILL.

DAY II

FASTING AS JESUS FASTED

Scripture Reading: Luke 4:14 (NIV)

FASTING FOR STRENGTH AND FOCUS
"Jesus returned to Galilee in the power of the Spirit, and news about him spread through the whole countryside."

REFLECTION:
After His fast, Jesus returned empowered by the Holy Spirit. Fasting not only helps us to disconnect from the physical but also to reconnect with God in a deeper way. It provides clarity and strength for the tasks and challenges ahead. Just as Jesus emerged from His fast with renewed power and purpose, our fast can also lead to spiritual rejuvenation and a clearer sense of God's direction.

PRAYER:
Father, I ask for Your strength and focus during this fast. Let Your Spirit empower and guide me in all that I do. Help me to remain steadfast and to experience Your power in new ways. Amen.

CONTEMPLATION:
Consider an area in your life where you need spiritual strength or clarity. Pray specifically about this area, and ask God to use your fast to provide insight and empowerment.

Aligning Your Thoughts

Date

YOU WERE NOT CREATED BY ACCIDENT, BUT DESIGNED
WITH DIVINE PRECISION FOR A PURPOSE ONLY YOU CAN FULFILL.

DAY III

FASTING AS JESUS FASTED

Scripture Reading: Matthew 4:3-4 (NIV)

OVERCOMING TEMPTATION THROUGH FASTING

"The tempter came to him and said, 'If you are the Son of God, tell these stones to become bread.' Jesus answered, 'It is written: 'Man shall not live on bread alone, but on every word that comes from the mouth of God.''"

REFLECTION:

During His fast, Jesus was tempted by the devil, but He countered each temptation with the Word of God. Fasting can be a powerful way to strengthen our resistance to temptation. By focusing on spiritual nourishment rather than physical, we align ourselves more closely with God's Word and find strength to overcome the trials and temptations we face.

PRAYER:

Lord, as I fast, help me to rely on Your Word for strength and guidance. Help me to resist temptation and to find my sustenance in You alone. Amen.

CONTEMPLATION:

Identify a specific temptation or struggle you face. Pray about this issue, and ask God to give you strength to overcome it during your fast.

Aligning Your Thoughts

Date
....

YOU WERE NOT CREATED BY ACCIDENT, BUT DESIGNED
WITH DIVINE PRECISION FOR A PURPOSE ONLY YOU CAN FULFILL.

DAY IV

FASTING AS JESUS FASTED

Scripture Reading: Matthew 6:16-18 (NIV)

THE ATTITUDE OF THE HEART

"When you fast, do not look somber as the hypocrites do, for they disfigure their faces to show others they are fasting. Truly I tell you, they have received their reward in full. But when you fast, anoint your head and wash your face, so that it will not be obvious to others that you are fasting, but only to your Father, who is unseen; and your Father, who sees what is done in secret, will reward you."

REFLECTION:

Jesus teaches that the attitude of our heart is crucial when fasting. It should be a private and humble act of devotion rather than a public display. Fasting is about your personal relationship with God, not about showing off to others. Cultivating a sincere heart and focusing on God rather than on how others perceive your fast will deepen the spiritual impact of this practice.

PRAYER:

Lord, help me to approach this fast with a humble heart. May my focus be on You alone, and may I not seek approval or recognition from others. Teach me to seek Your presence above all. Amen.

CONTEMPLATION:

Evaluate your attitude towards fasting. Are there any areas where you might be seeking validation from others? Pray for a pure heart and renewed focus on God.

Date

....

YOU WERE NOT CREATED BY ACCIDENT, BUT DESIGNED
WITH DIVINE PRECISION FOR A PURPOSE ONLY YOU CAN FULFILL.

DAY V

FASTING AS JESUS FASTED

Scripture Reading: Isaiah 58:6-7 (NIV)

THE FRUIT OF FASTING

"'Is not this the kind of fasting I have chosen: to loose the chains of injustice and untie the cords of the yoke, to set the oppressed free and break every yoke? Is it not to share your food with the hungry and to provide the poor wanderer with shelter—when you see the naked, to clothe them, and not to turn away from your own flesh and blood?'"

REFLECTION:

Fasting is not just a personal spiritual exercise, but it also leads to
outward expressions of love and justice. God desires our fasting to produce the fruit of compassion and justice in the world. It's a time to not
only seek personal spiritual renewal but to reach out and serve others, reflecting God's love through our actions.

PRAYER:

Father, let the fruit of my fasting be evident in my actions towards others. Help me use this time to serve those in need and to act justly. May my fast bring about tangible expressions of Your love and compassion. Amen.

CONTEMPLATION:

Think about ways you can serve others during your fast. Plan one specific act of kindness or service that reflects the compassion and justice God desires.

Date

YOU WERE NOT CREATED BY ACCIDENT, BUT DESIGNED
WITH DIVINE PRECISION FOR A PURPOSE ONLY YOU CAN FULFILL.

WHOLENESS COMES FROM ALIGNMENT

THIS IS PLUMB

God's Word is my measuring line for healing and truth.

THIS IS NOT

I can fix myself with self-help or comparison.

"He sent out his word and healed them..." – Psalm 107:20

CLOSING JOURNAL:

FASTING LIKE JESUS

1. REFLECTION ON THE FAST
What did I choose to fast from and why?
How did fasting help me focus on God this week?
Were there moments where I struggled? How did I overcome them?

2. SPIRITUAL GROWTH
What has God revealed to me about His character or my walk with Him
during this time of fasting?
How has fasting strengthened my faith or dependence on God?
In what ways did I experience spiritual breakthrough or clarity?

3. ALIGNING WITH JESUS' EXAMPLE
How did I emulate Jesus' humility, obedience, or reliance on God during
this time?
What have I learned about the purpose and power of fasting through His
example?
How did fasting draw me closer to God's heart and mission?

4. GRATITUDE AND AWARENESS
List three blessings or lessons I've gained through this fast.
How did I sense God's presence and provision this week?

5. CLOSING PRAYER
Write a prayer of thanksgiving for God's guidance, asking Him to
continue shaping your heart and strengthening your discipline.

6. VISION FOR THE FUTURE
What changes will I carry forward to stay aligned with God's will and
deepen my
walk with Him?

This prompt invites deep reflection on the spiritual, emotional, and
practical aspects of fasting, encouraging personal growth and alignment
with Jesus' example.

Aligning Your Thoughts

YOU WERE NOT CREATED BY ACCIDENT, BUT DESIGNED
WITH DIVINE PRECISION FOR A PURPOSE ONLY YOU CAN FULFILL.

SPEAKING

GOD'S WORD TO MOVE MOUNTAINS

PURPOSE REVEALED

MY JOURNEY TO FREEDOM: HOW GOD'S WORD TRANSFORMED MY LIFE

In the early days of my faith journey, I uncovered a life-changing truth: my identity in Christ and the authority I carry as a believer. As I dove deeper into Scripture, I realized God's Word wasn't just meant to be read. It was meant to be declared.

At first, it felt awkward. I remember pacing around my house, speaking verses aloud like battle cries against the chaos in my mind. Psalm 91 became my anchor: "He who dwells in the secret place of the Most High shall abide under the shadow of the Almighty." I clung to it as I fought through depression, anxiety, and the weight of past trauma.

For most of my life, I believed that pain and confusion were just part of who I was. II didn't realize how much my unstable childhood had shaped my identity in ways I never thought to question. But then... God stepped in.

As I immersed myself in God's Word, I began to see the truth: I didn't have to stay stuck. Depression, fear, and brokenness were not my inheritance. I saw myself in the stories of women throughout Scripture—the ones desperate for healing, for hope, for something real. And I started to believe that God's promises were for me, too.

I began to pray Scripture and speak God's promises over my life. Slowly but surely, things started to shift. I began waking up without the heavy weight that once kept me in bed. I felt peace in public spaces instead of anxiety. I noticed beauty around me—things I had long overlooked. Even the physical tension in my body began to lift, as spiritual and physical healing unfolded side by side.

PURPOSE REVEALED

But more than anything, I experienced a supernatural peace. It was the kind that surpasses all understanding. It was like the fog cleared, and for the first time,
I could see. Romans 10:17 became real to me: "Faith comes by hearing, and hearing by the word of God."

God's Word didn't just change how I thought. It changed my life.

And I want you to know this: it can do the same for you. No matter what you're facing—depression, anxiety, pain, or your past—God's Word has the power to
move mountains. I'm living proof that when you declare His Word in faith, everything can change.

DAY I

SPEAKING GOD'S WORD TO MOVE MOUNTAINS

Scripture Reading: Isaiah 55:11 (NIV)

THE POWER OF GOD'S WORD

"So shall my word be that goes out from my mouth; it shall not return to me empty, but it shall accomplish that which I purpose, and shall succeed in the thing for which I sent it."

REFLECTION:

God's Word is powerful and purposeful. It is never empty or ineffective but always accomplishes His will. Reflect on how God's Word has worked in your life or in the lives of others to bring about transformation, healing, or guidance. Consider the many ways Scripture has impacted people throughout history and how it continues to carry out God's purposes today.

PRAYER:

Lord, thank You for the power and effectiveness of Your Word. Help me to understand and apply it more deeply in my life. May Your Word address the challenges I face and bring me closer to Your will. Teach me to rely on Your Word to guide me in every situation. Amen.

CONTEMPLATION:

Read a passage of Scripture that speaks to a specific challenge you're facing. Reflect on how this passage shows God's power and purpose.
Write a prayer thanking God for His Word and asking Him to help you apply it in your life.

Aligning Your Thoughts

Date

YOU WERE NOT CREATED BY ACCIDENT, BUT DESIGNED
WITH DIVINE PRECISION FOR A PURPOSE ONLY YOU CAN FULFILL.

DAY II

SPEAKING GOD'S WORD TO MOVE MOUNTAINS

Scripture Reading: James 5:14-15 (NIV)

SPEAKING TO ILLNESS

"Is anyone among you sick?
Let them call the elders of the church to pray over them and
anoint them with oil in the name of the Lord. And
the prayer offered in faith will make the sick person well;
the Lord will raise them up."

REFLECTION:

Faith and prayer in the name of Jesus have the power to
bring healing. Reflect on how speaking God's Word can
strengthen your prayers for those who are ill. Consider how
Scripture, which promises healing, can be a source of comfort
and faith in times of sickness. Through prayer, we can align
ourselves with God's will and trust in His power to heal and
restore.

PRAYER:

Lord, I lift up those who are sick and in need of healing. I
speak Your Word over them, asking for Your healing touch
and restoration. May Your will be done, and may they
experience Your power and grace in their lives. I trust in Your
ability to heal according to Your perfect plan. Amen.

CONTEMPLATION:

Identify someone who is ill, and commit to praying for them
using Scripture that promises healing. Write a prayer based
on God's Word for their situation, speaking His truth and
trusting in His healing power.

Aligning Your Thoughts

YOU WERE NOT CREATED BY ACCIDENT, BUT DESIGNED
WITH DIVINE PRECISION FOR A PURPOSE ONLY YOU CAN FULFILL.

DAY III

SPEAKING GOD'S WORD TO MOVE MOUNTAINS

Scripture Reading: Matthew 17:20 (NIV)

ADDRESSING TROUBLES AND CHALLENGES

"He replied, 'Because you have so little faith. Truly I tell you, if you have faith as small as a mustard seed, you can say to this mountain, "Move from here to there," and it will move. Nothing will be impossible for you.'"

REFLECTION:

Jesus teaches that even faith as small as a mustard seed has the power to move mountains. Reflect on the challenges in your life that seem insurmountable, and consider how speaking God's Word can help you change your perspective and approach. God's promises give us the authority to address obstacles and trust in His ability to overcome them.

PRAYER:

Lord, I ask You to increase my faith and help me trust in Your promises. Give me the strength to speak Your Word with authority and believe that You can move mountains in my life. Help me to rely on You when facing obstacles and to remember that nothing is impossible for You. Amen.

CONTEMPLATION:

Write down one major challenge you are currently facing. Find a Scripture that speaks to overcoming such challenges, and declare it out loud, affirming your faith in God's ability to handle it. Keep this Scripture in your heart as a reminder of His power and faithfulness.

Aligning Your Thoughts

Date

YOU WERE NOT CREATED BY ACCIDENT, BUT DESIGNED
WITH DIVINE PRECISION FOR A PURPOSE ONLY YOU CAN FULFILL.

DAY IV

SPEAKING GOD'S WORD TO MOVE MOUNTAINS

Scripture Reading: 1 John 5:14-15 (NIV)

ALIGNING WITH GOD'S WILL
"This is the confidence we have in approaching God: that if we ask anything according to his will, he hears us. And if we know that he hears us—whatever we ask—we know that we have what we asked of him."

REFLECTION:
Praying and speaking in alignment with God's will ensures that our prayers are effective. Reflect on how aligning your words and requests with His will can strengthen your confidence and faith in the outcome of your prayers. When we align ourselves with God's purpose, we can trust that He will answer according to His good and perfect plan.

PRAYER:
Lord, help me to align my words and prayers with Your will. Guide me to understand Your purpose and speak in faith, trusting that You hear me and will answer according to Your perfect plan. Strengthen my confidence in Your promises, knowing You always do what is best. Amen.

CONTEMPLATION:
Choose a prayer or declaration you've been making and evaluate it against Scripture to ensure it aligns with God's will. Adjust your words as needed, and pray for confirmation that your requests are in line with His purpose.

Date
____

YOU WERE NOT CREATED BY ACCIDENT, BUT DESIGNED
WITH DIVINE PRECISION FOR A PURPOSE ONLY YOU CAN FULFILL.

DAY V

SPEAKING GOD'S WORD TO MOVE MOUNTAINS

Scripture Reading: Joshua 1:8 (NIV)

THE SUCCESS OF GOD'S WORD

"Keep this Book of the Law always on your lips; meditate on it day and night, so that you may be careful to do everything written in it. Then you will be prosperous and successful."

REFLECTION:

God's Word is guaranteed to accomplish His purposes. Reflect on how meditating on and speaking His Word daily leads to fulfillment in His plan. Consider how God promises prosperity not just in material terms but in spiritual growth, obedience, and alignment with His will. Speaking and living out His Word brings true victory .

PRAYER:

Lord, thank You for the promise that Your Word will not return empty but will accomplish all that You intend. Help me to delight in Your Word and to live according to its truth. May my life reflect the success and prosperity that comes from living in obedience to Your Word. Amen.

CONTEMPLATION:

Choose a promise from Scripture that speaks to your current situation and commit to speaking it over your life daily. Meditate on this promise, trusting that God will bring about its success in His perfect timing.

Date

YOU WERE NOT CREATED BY ACCIDENT, BUT DESIGNED
WITH DIVINE PRECISION FOR A PURPOSE ONLY YOU CAN FULFILL.

HIDDEN SEASONS
ARE
HOLY TOO

THIS IS PLUMB

God does sacred work in quiet seasons.

THIS IS NOT

If I'm not seen, I'm not significant.

"He made everything beautiful in its time..."
– Ecclesiastes 3:11

CLOSING JOURNAL:

SPEAKING GOD'S WORD TO MOVE MOUNTAINS

1. REFLECTION ON THE WEEK

What "mountains" (challenges or obstacles) did I face this week?
How did I respond to these challenges with God's Word or
declarations?
Were there moments when I struggled to speak faith or truth? How
did I overcome them?

2. POWER OF GOD'S WORD

How did speaking God's Word impact my thoughts, emotions, or
circumstances this week? What scriptures did I declare over my life or
situations?
How did I witness God's power at work through His Word in my life?

3. TRUSTING IN GOD'S PROMISES

How has my faith in God's promises grown this week?
Were there any specific promises from the Bible that stood out to me
and gave
me strength?
In what ways have I seen God respond to my declarations of faith?

4. GRATITUDE FOR GOD'S WORD

List three ways God's Word has brought clarity, peace, or
breakthrough.
How have I experienced God's faithfulness as I've spoken His Word
over my situations?

5. PRAYER FOR BOLDNESS

Write a prayer asking God to continue strengthening your faith and
boldness to
speak His Word with authority in every situation.

CLOSING JOURNAL:

Speaking God's Word to Move Mountains

6. Vision for the Future

What specific area of my life do I need to speak God's Word over in
the coming week
to see mountains moved?

This prompt encourages deep reflection on the power of speaking
God's Word, growth in faith, and a commitment to applying God's
promises with confidence moving forward.

Date

YOU WERE NOT CREATED BY ACCIDENT, BUT DESIGNED
WITH DIVINE PRECISION FOR A PURPOSE ONLY YOU CAN FULFILL.

SPIRITUAL
WARFARE

PURPOSE REVEALED

SPIRITUAL WARFARE

During a season I believed to be led by the Holy Spirit, I entered into a time of intense prayer, fasting, worship, and deep study of God's Word. While I always strive to be Spirit-led, this particular decision didn't make sense on paper. Our family was thriving financially, and I had just been offered a promotion that could have advanced our version of a "good life." But I turned it down. Instead, I quit my job—fully convinced that God was calling me to set everything aside so I could seek Him with undivided attention. During that time, the frequency of dreams increased. And one stood out as a clear warning.

In the dream, I came home to find that the plants in my house had been moved or re-potted. One of my favorites had been relocated to another room. I asked my brother-in-law—who is a pastor and was visiting our family—"Do you know who's been moving my plants?" I thought maybe my mother-in-law, a plant lover, had done it. Then, walking into the furthest room at the back of the house, I saw many plants neglected and covered in cobwebs—fading and forgotten. I felt an urgency to clean and revive them. But just as I turned to gather supplies, a deadly spider crawled onto my shoulder, aiming to bite my neck and stop me.

When I woke up, I knew God was showing me something critical. Because I had postured myself to seek Him wholeheartedly, He began rearranging things in my life, bringing to light areas that needed His healing. The neglected plants symbolized parts of my life, especially in my marriage, that had gone unattended. The spider was the enemy's attempt to prevent healing and restoration.

God was moving the life-giving things in my home—symbolizing spiritual growth and His provision. He was re-potting what needed new soil, revealing where the enemy had quietly worked to destroy. And yet, I didn't have to fight alone. Because I had been at Jesus' feet, He was the one exposing the enemy's schemes and fighting for me.

PURPOSE REVEALED

SPIRITUAL WARFARE

That dream taught me something profound: spiritual warfare isn't always loud or dramatic. Sometimes, the greatest battles are fought through quiet surrender and unwavering devotion. Sitting at the feet of Jesus—seeking His will, not our own—is where true victory begins. He fights for us, reveals what's hidden, and restores what's broken.

Now, I look at the "plants" in my life—some thriving, some needing care—and see symbols of God's ongoing work. It's not my strength, but His faithfulness that brings healing, growth, and victory. He is the gardener of my soul, and when I seek Him, He always tends to what matters most.

DAY I

SPIRITUAL WARFARE

Scripture Reading: Ephesians 6:10-12 (NIV)

UNDERSTANDING THE BATTLE

"Finally, be strong in the Lord and in his mighty power. Put on the full armor of God, so that you can take your stand against the devil's schemes. For our struggle is not against flesh and blood, but against the rulers, against the authorities, against the powers of this dark world and against the spiritual forces of evil in the heavenly realms."

REFLECTION:

Spiritual warfare is a fundamental aspect of the Christian walk. Unlike physical battles, this struggle is not against people but against spiritual forces that seek to disrupt our relationship with God. These forces are at work behind the scenes, influencing our thoughts, emotions, and circumstances. By recognizing that our struggles are not merely physical or emotional but are spiritual in nature, we can stand firm with the armor of God—His Word, faith, righteousness, and peace. With the right tools, we can confront and overcome the enemy's schemes.

PRAYER:

Heavenly Father, help me understand the nature of the spiritual battle I am in. Open my eyes to the schemes of the enemy and give me the wisdom to discern when spiritual warfare is at play. Strengthen me to stand firm in Your power, and equip me to overcome the forces of darkness with Your armor. Amen.

CONTEMPLATION:

Reflect on a challenge or situation where you may have been focused solely on the physical or emotional aspects. Write a prayer asking God to reveal the spiritual dimensions of that situation and to give you the strength and tools to fight with His power.

Date
....

YOU WERE NOT CREATED BY ACCIDENT, BUT DESIGNED
WITH DIVINE PRECISION FOR A PURPOSE ONLY YOU CAN FULFILL.

DAY II

SPIRITUAL WARFARE

Scripture Reading: Ephesians 6:13-17 (NIV)

THE ARMOR OF GOD
"Therefore put on the full armor of God, so that when the day of evil comes, you may be able to stand your ground, and after you have done everything, to stand. Stand firm then, with the belt of truth buckled around your waist, with the breastplate of righteousness in place, and with your feet fitted with the readiness that comes from the gospel of peace. In addition to all this, take up the shield of faith, with which you can extinguish all the flaming arrows of the evil one. Take the helmet of salvation and the sword of the Spirit, which is the word of God."

DEVOTIONAL THOUGHT:
God has provided us with spiritual armor to defend against the attacks of the enemy. Each piece of armor has a specific role: truth to counter lies, righteousness to guard our hearts, peace to steady our steps, faith to protect against doubts, salvation to secure our minds, and the Word of God as our offensive weapon. Embracing and utilizing this armor is crucial in our daily spiritual battles.

PRAYER:
Lord, I put on Your armor today. Help me to live in truth, righteousness, peace, faith, and salvation. Equip me with Your Word so that I can effectively counter the enemy's attacks. Amen.

Aligning Your Thoughts

Date

YOU WERE NOT CREATED BY ACCIDENT, BUT DESIGNED
WITH DIVINE PRECISION FOR A PURPOSE ONLY YOU CAN FULFILL.

DAY III

SPIRITUAL WARFARE

Scripture Reading: Ephesians 6:18 (NIV)

THE POWER OF PRAYER

"And pray in the Spirit on all occasions with all kinds of prayers and requests. With this in mind, be alert and always keep on praying for all
the Lord's people."

REFLECTION:

Prayer is a powerful weapon in spiritual warfare. It connects us directly to God, allowing us to align our hearts with His will and bringing divine intervention into our lives and the lives of others. Through prayer, we invite God's strength and presence to guide, protect, and empower us in our spiritual battles. It is not just about asking for help, but about staying alert and being responsive to the Holy Spirit's leading. Prayer strengthens our defenses, shields us from the enemy's tactics, and advances God's kingdom on earth.

PRAYER:

Father, teach me to pray with vigilance and sincerity. Help me stay alert and consistent in my prayers, not only for myself but for others.
May my prayers be a powerful force that resists the enemy's schemes and brings about Your will. Amen.

CONTEMPLATION:

Reflect on a recent challenge or temptation you faced. Write a prayer asking God for His intervention and guidance in that situation, committing to pray with greater vigilance and sincerity in the future.

Aligning Your Thoughts

Date
____

YOU WERE NOT CREATED BY ACCIDENT, BUT DESIGNED
WITH DIVINE PRECISION FOR A PURPOSE ONLY YOU CAN FULFILL.

DAY IV

SPIRITUAL WARFARE

Scripture Reading: 1 Peter 5:8-9 (NIV)

THE ROLE OF FAITH AND TRUST

"Be alert and of sober mind. Your enemy the devil prowls around like a roaring lion looking for someone to devour. Resist him, standing firm in the faith, because you know that the family of believers throughout the world is undergoing the same kind of sufferings."

REFLECTION:

Faith and trust in God are essential in resisting the devil's attacks. The enemy seeks to create fear and doubt, but standing firm in faith means trusting in God's promises and His power over all things. When we face trials, it's important to remember that we are not alone. Believers around the world are undergoing similar struggles, and by encouraging one another in the faith, we can strengthen our collective resistance against the enemy. Trusting God's faithfulness helps us remain steadfast, even in the face of adversity.

PRAYER:

Lord, increase my faith and help me stand firm in Your promises. Remind me that I am not alone in this battle and strengthen me to resist the enemy with unwavering trust in You. Amen.

CONTEMPLATION:

Think of a recent trial where you felt tempted to give in to doubt or fear. Write a prayer reaffirming your trust in God's power and His promises. Ask Him to strengthen your faith and help you stand firm against the enemy's attacks.

Date
....

YOU WERE NOT CREATED BY ACCIDENT, BUT DESIGNED
WITH DIVINE PRECISION FOR A PURPOSE ONLY YOU CAN FULFILL.

DAY V

SPIRITUAL WARFARE

Scripture Reading: Revelation 12:10-11 (NIV)

VICTORY IN CHRIST

"Then I heard a loud voice in heaven say: 'Now have come the salvation and the power and the kingdom of our God, and the authority of his Messiah. For the accuser of our brothers and sisters, who accuses them before our God day and night, has been hurled down. They triumphed over him by the blood of the Lamb and by the word of their testimony; they did not love their lives so much as to shrink from death.'"

REFLECTION:

Our ultimate victory in spiritual warfare is secured through the blood of Jesus Christ. The enemy may continue to accuse and attack us, but Christ has already defeated him. While we may face battles in this life, we can stand firm in the power and authority of Jesus, who has already overcome the enemy. Our testimonies, rooted in His sacrifice, are powerful tools in overcoming the lies and accusations of the accuser. Living in the light of this victory enables us to face challenges with unwavering confidence and hope, knowing that we are more than conquerors in Christ.

PRAYER:

Thank You, Jesus, for Your victory over sin and the enemy. Help me live in the reality of this victory, trusting in Your power and proclaiming Your truth. May my life reflect the triumph You have won for me. Amen.

CONTEMPLATION:

Reflect on a specific area where you've experienced the enemy's accusations or attacks. Write a prayer declaring the victory of Christ over that area and proclaiming your trust in His power to overcome all opposition.

Aligning Your Thoughts

Date

YOU WERE NOT CREATED BY ACCIDENT, BUT DESIGNED
WITH DIVINE PRECISION FOR A PURPOSE ONLY YOU CAN FULFILL.

THE PLUMB LINE ISN'T PERFECTION

THIS IS PLUMB

God desires alignment, not perfection.

THIS IS NOT

If I mess up, I'm disqualified.

"My grace is sufficient for you, for my power is made perfect in weakness." – 2 Corinthians 12:9

CLOSING JOURNAL:

SPIRITUAL WARFARE

1. REFLECTION ON THE WEEK
What battles did I face this week, and how did I respond in God's strength? When I felt overwhelmed, how did I fight back with His truth?

2. ARMOR OF GOD
How did I put on the armor of God this week (Ephesians 6:10-18)? Which piece of the armor stood out to me, and how did it help me in the fight?
In what areas did I need to rely more on God's protection and power?

3. VICTORY IN CHRIST
How did I experience victory over the enemy this week?
Were there moments where I had to remind myself of God's victory over spiritual forces?
What scriptures or truths did I speak to strengthen myself in battle?

4. STRENGTHENING MY FAITH
How was my faith strengthened in battle? How did God show His faithfulness in protecting or delivering me, and how did challenges deepen my reliance on Him

5. GRATITUDE AND AWARENESS
List three ways God has fought on my behalf this week.
How have I experienced God's presence and peace in the midst of battle?

6. PRAYER FOR PROTECTION AND STRENGTH
Write a prayer asking God to continue to equip you for spiritual warfare, to guard your mind, heart, and spirit, and to deepen your trust in His power.

7. PREPARING FOR THE FUTURE
What area of my life should I strengthen this week to stand firm against spiritual attacks?

This prompt encourages reflection on the battle against spiritual forces, the use of God's armor, and a deepening understanding of victory through Christ. It also prepares you for future spiritual battles with faith and confidence.

Date
____

YOU WERE NOT CREATED BY ACCIDENT, BUT DESIGNED
WITH DIVINE PRECISION FOR A PURPOSE ONLY YOU CAN FULFILL.

THE GLORY & POWER

OF THE LIVING WORD, JESUS

PURPOSE REVEALED

Encountering Scripture as a Living, Breathing Relationship

There is nothing more life-altering, perspective-shifting, and soul-renewing than the **living Word—Jesus**. He's not just the written words of Scripture; He is the embodiment of truth, the breath of heaven, and the ultimate revelation of the Father's heart.

In seasons where I've felt lost, confused, or weighed down by life, it wasn't simply encouragement that rescued me. It was the Word. The Word that speaks life into dead places. The Word that cuts through the noise and brings clarity.
The Word that is alive, active, and never returns void.

When I began to treat Scripture not just as something to read, but as Someone to encounter, everything changed. The Word became nourishment to my soul, direction for my path, and power for my battles. **Jesus, the Living Word**, meets us right where we are, and through His presence, we are transformed.

This section of the devotional is meant to help you encounter the Word not as information, but as revelation. Let it awaken your spirit. Let it confront lies and heal wounds. Let it restore your identity and revive your purpose.

If you've been spiritually dry, disconnected, or distracted, return to the Word—
not just for answers, but for communion. Sit with it. Soak in it. Allow the Spirit to breathe through every verse until your heart beats in rhythm with His. "In the beginning was the Word, and the Word was with God, and the Word was God…
The Word became flesh and made His dwelling among us" (John 1:1, 14).
Jesus is the Living Word—and when we open the Word, we are opening ourselves to Him.

DAY I

GLORY & POWER OF THE LIVING WORD, JESUS

Scripture Reading: John 1:1-3 (NIV)

THE WORD THAT CREATES
"In the beginning was the Word, and the Word was with God, and the Word was God. He was with God in the beginning. Through him all things were made; without him nothing was made that has been made."

REFLECTION:
Jesus, as the Living Word, holds creative power. Everything that exists was brought into being through Him. This demonstrates His divine authority and majesty. The same power that created the universe is active in our lives today, shaping and sustaining us.

PRAYER:
Lord Jesus, You are the Word through whom all things were created. I praise You for Your power and majesty. Help me to trust in Your creative power and recognize Your hand in every aspect of my life. Amen.

CONTEMPLATION:
Reflect on the aspects of your life where you need to see Jesus' creative power at work. Ask God to reveal His creative solutions and sustaining presence in those areas.

Aligning Your Thoughts

Date ....

YOU WERE NOT CREATED BY ACCIDENT, BUT DESIGNED
WITH DIVINE PRECISION FOR A PURPOSE ONLY YOU CAN FULFILL.

DAY II

GLORY & POWER OF THE LIVING WORD, JESUS

Scripture Reading: John 1:4-5 (NIV)

THE WORD THAT HEALS

Scripture Reading: Matthew 8:16-17 (NIV)
"When evening came, many who were demon-possessed were brought to him, and he drove out the spirits with a word and healed all the sick.
This was to fulfill what was spoken through the prophet Isaiah:
"He took up our infirmities and bore our diseases.""

REFLECTION:

The power of Jesus as the Living Word extends to healing and deliverance. His words bring physical and spiritual restoration. He fulfills the prophecy by bearing our infirmities and diseases, demonstrating His compassion and divine authority over all sickness.

PRAYER:

Jesus, thank You for Your healing power. I bring before You my own needs and the needs of those I love. Speak Your word of healing and restoration into our lives. May Your power be evident in our physical, emotional, and spiritual well-being. Amen.

CONTEMPLATION:

Identify areas in your life, or in the lives of others, where you need healing. Pray specifically for Jesus' intervention and healing power to be at work.

Aligning Your Thoughts

Date

YOU WERE NOT CREATED BY ACCIDENT, BUT DESIGNED
WITH DIVINE PRECISION FOR A PURPOSE ONLY YOU CAN FULFILL.

DAY III

GLORY & POWER OF THE LIVING WORD, JESUS

Scripture Reading: 2 Corinthians 5:17 (NIV)

THE WORD THAT TRANSFORMS

"Therefore, if anyone is in Christ, the new creation has come: The old has gone, the new is here!"

REFLECTION:

The Living Word has the power to transform our lives completely. When we are in Christ, we become new creations. This transformation is not merely superficial but deeply affects our entire being, renewing our mind, heart, and purpose.

PRAYER:

Lord Jesus, thank You for the transformative power of Your Word. Help me to embrace my identity as a new creation in You. Renew my mind and heart, and guide me to live out the new life You have given me. Amen.

CONTEMPLATION:

Consider areas in your life where you desire transformation. Seek Jesus' power to renew and change those aspects, asking for His guidance and strength in the process.

Aligning Your Thoughts

Date ____________________

DAY IV

GLORY & POWER OF THE LIVING WORD, JESUS

Scripture Reading: Psalm 119:105 (NIV)

THE WORD THAT GUIDES
"Your word is a lamp for my feet, a light on my path."

REFLECTION:
Jesus, as the Living Word, provides guidance and illumination for our journey. His words are a source of wisdom and direction, helping us navigate life's uncertainties. Embracing His guidance ensures that we
walk in His ways and fulfill His purposes.

PRAYER:
Lord, thank You for being the light and guide in my life. Illuminate my path with Your Word and direct my steps according to Your will. Help me to trust in Your guidance and to follow You faithfully. Amen.

CONTEMPLATION:
Reflect on a decision you are facing. Pray for Jesus' guidance and clarity, asking Him to shed light on your path and lead you according to His will.

Aligning Your Thoughts

Date
____

YOU WERE NOT CREATED BY ACCIDENT, BUT DESIGNED
WITH DIVINE PRECISION FOR A PURPOSE ONLY YOU CAN FULFILL.

DAY V

GLORY & POWER OF THE LIVING WORD, JESUS

Scripture Reading: Acts 1:8 (NIV)

THE WORD THAT EMPOWERS

"But you will receive power when the Holy Spirit comes on you; and you will be my witnesses in Jerusalem, and in all Judea and Samaria, and to the ends of the earth."

REFLECTION:

The Living Word not only creates, heals, transforms, and guides but also empowers us for service. Through the Holy Spirit, Jesus grants us power to be His witnesses and to live out His mission. This empowerment equips us to spread His message and embody His love.

PRAYER:

Jesus, thank You for the power You give through the Holy Spirit. Empower me to be a witness of Your love and truth in my community and beyond. Fill me with Your strength to carry out Your mission in the world. Amen.

CONTEMPLATION:

Think about how you can use the power Jesus gives you to impact those around you. Pray for opportunities and boldness to be a witness of His love and power in your daily life.

Date

YOU WERE NOT CREATED BY ACCIDENT, BUT DESIGNED
WITH DIVINE PRECISION FOR A PURPOSE ONLY YOU CAN FULFILL.

CALLING ISN'T A PLATFORM

THIS IS PLUMB

I'm called to faithfulness, not fame.

THIS IS NOT

Purpose is only found on a big stage.

"Whatever you do, do it all for the glory of God." – 1 Corinthians 10:31

CLOSING JOURNAL:

THE GLORY & POWER OF THE LIVING WORD, JESUS

1. REFLECTION ON THE GLORY OF JESUS

How did I encounter Jesus' glory this week—in His majesty, splendor, presence, or power?

2. ENCOUNTERING THE LIVING WORD

How did my understanding of Jesus as the Living Word deepen this week through Scripture, and how did it transform me?

3. THE POWER OF JESUS IN MY LIFE

In what areas of my life did I witness the power of Jesus at work?
How did I rely on His strength or authority in difficult situations?
How did Jesus' power bring healing, peace, or breakthrough in my heart or circumstances?

4. WORSHIP AND REVERENCE

How did I worship or honor Jesus this week in response to His glory and power?
What new perspective have I gained about the relationship between Jesus, the Word,
and my daily life?

5. GRATITUDE AND AWE

List three ways I've seen God's glory or Jesus' power revealed in my life this week.
How has the presence of the Living Word made a difference in my journey?

CLOSING JOURNAL:

6. Prayer of Adoration and Surrender

Write a prayer of adoration for Jesus, acknowledging His glory and power as the Living Word. Ask for a deeper understanding and experience of His presence in the week ahead.

7. Moving Forward in the Power of the Word

How can I carry the glory and power of Jesus with me into the next week? What steps can I take to remain rooted in the Living Word?

This journaling prompt helps you reflect on the power, glory, and transformative nature of Jesus as the Living Word, encouraging worship, gratitude, and a commitment to live in His presence and power moving forward.

Date
....

YOU WERE NOT CREATED BY ACCIDENT, BUT DESIGNED
WITH DIVINE PRECISION FOR A PURPOSE ONLY YOU CAN FULFILL.

THE POWER OF WORSHIP IN DAILY LIFE

PURPOSE REVEALED

"The Heart of Worship: Where My Soul Finds Home"

During a season when I was desperate to hear God's voice, I discovered that worship was not just something I did in church on Sundays—it became the atmosphere of my home and my heart. I had entered a time of deep prayer, fasting, and devotion, but it was in worship that I found myself most broken open before Him. Worship became my anchor. When fear pressed in, I lifted my voice and felt His peace. When discouragement whispered lies, worship realigned me to His truth. It wasn't about the music or the words, but about surrendering my whole being in reverence before the One who made me.

God began showing me that worship is more than singing—it is warfare. In worship, I laid down my burdens and picked up His strength. In worship, chains I couldn't break on my own fell away. In worship, I met Jesus face-to-face and experienced His presence in a way that no earthly thing could provide.

That season taught me something profound: worship is both a weapon and a love offering. It silences the enemy and heals the heart. It turns our eyes from the weight of this world to the glory of the Lord. And in that posture, God moves—He restores, He renews, and He reminds us that He alone is worthy.

These words flowed from a quiet moment of worship, capturing the essence of surrender and intimacy with God.

I Worship to worship
Bearing my soul
For the One who sees it
Makes it whole

— Michel Hernandez

"God is spirit, and his worshipers must worship in the Spirit and in truth." — John 4:24

DAY I

The Power of Worship in Daily Life

Scripture Reading: John 4:24 (NIV)

The Heart of Worship

"God is spirit, and his worshipers must worship in the Spirit and in truth."

Reflection:

Worship is not just about singing songs or attending church services; it is a heartfelt response to who God is. True worship happens when we engage our spirit and align our hearts with the truth of God's nature and His promises. It's a daily commitment to recognize and honor God's presence in all aspects of our lives.

Prayer:

Lord, help me to worship You with sincerity and truth. May my worship be a genuine reflection of my love and reverence for You, both in my heart and through my actions. Amen.

Contemplation:

Reflect on what worship means to you personally. Write down ways you can begin to worship God more authentically and consistently in your daily life.

Aligning Your Thoughts

Date

YOU WERE NOT CREATED BY ACCIDENT, BUT DESIGNED
WITH DIVINE PRECISION FOR A PURPOSE ONLY YOU CAN FULFILL.

DAY II

THE POWER OF WORSHIP IN DAILY LIFE

Scripture Reading: Colossians 3:23-24 (NIV)

WORSHIP THROUGH EVERYDAY ACTIONS

"Whatever you do, work at it with all your heart, as working for the Lord, not for human masters, since you know that you will receive an inheritance from the Lord as a reward. It is the Lord Christ you are serving."

REFLECTION:

Worship extends beyond church services and prayer times; it encompasses our daily activities. When we perform our tasks with a heart dedicated to God, whether at work, home, or in our interactions, we are worshiping Him. Every action done with excellence and integrity is an act of worship.

PRAYER:

Father, help me to see every task and responsibility as an opportunity to worship You. Teach me to work with a heart of gratitude and dedication, honoring You in all that I do. Amen.

CONTEMPLATION:

Identify a daily activity or responsibility where you can improve your attitude or approach. Consider how you can turn this task into an act of worship by working with a heart devoted to God.

Aligning Your Thoughts

Date

DAY III

The Power of Worship in Daily Life

Scripture Reading: Hebrews 10:24-25 (NIV)

Worship in Community

"And let us consider how we may spur one another on toward love and good deeds, not giving up meeting together, as some are in the habit of doing, but encouraging one another —and all the more as you see the Day approaching."

Reflection:

Worship is not only a personal experience but also a communal one. Gathering with fellow believers provides encouragement and strengthens our collective worship. Sharing our experiences and supporting each other in faith helps us grow and deepen our worship as a community.

Prayer:

Lord, thank You for the gift of community. Help me to be an encourager and to participate actively in worship with others. May our gatherings be filled with Your presence and a source of mutual encouragement and growth. Amen.

Contemplation:

Think about your involvement in your church or faith community. Consider how you can contribute more to collective worship and support others in their spiritual journey.

Aligning Your Thoughts

Date ______________

YOU WERE NOT CREATED BY ACCIDENT, BUT DESIGNED
WITH DIVINE PRECISION FOR A PURPOSE ONLY YOU CAN FULFILL.

DAY IV

THE POWER OF WORSHIP IN DAILY LIFE

Scripture Reading: Acts 16:25 (NIV)

WORSHIP IN ADVERSITY

"About midnight Paul and Silas were praying and singing hymns to God, and the other prisoners were listening to them."

REFLECTION:

Worship can be particularly powerful in times of difficulty and adversity. Paul and Silas, despite being in prison, chose to worship God through prayer and song. Their worship not only strengthened their own spirits but also had an impact on those around them. Worship in tough times demonstrates our trust in God's sovereignty and can inspire others.

PRAYER:

Lord, help me to worship You even in challenging circumstances. Teach me to find strength and hope in You through every trial and to let my worship be a testament to Your faithfulness. Amen.

CONTEMPLATION:

Identify a current challenge or difficult situation in your life. Spend time in worship and prayer, asking God to give you strength and perspective to glorify Him even in this adversity.

Aligning Your Thoughts

Date

YOU WERE NOT CREATED BY ACCIDENT, BUT DESIGNED
WITH DIVINE PRECISION FOR A PURPOSE ONLY YOU CAN FULFILL.

DAY V

THE POWER OF WORSHIP IN DAILY LIFE

Scripture Reading: 2 Corinthians 3:18 (NIV)

THE TRANSFORMATIVE POWER OF WORSHIP

"And we all, who with unveiled faces contemplate the Lord's glory, are being transformed into his image with ever-increasing glory, which comes from the Lord, who is the Spirit."

REFLECTION:

Worship has a transformative power. As we focus on God's glory and majesty, we are gradually transformed into His likeness. This process of transformation involves a continual renewal of our hearts and minds, aligning us more closely with His will and character.

PRAYER:

Father, I desire to be transformed by Your presence. As I worship, may Your Spirit work in me to shape my character and reflect Your image. Help me to embrace this process of transformation and grow in Your likeness. Amen.

CONTEMPLATION:

Reflect on how worship has impacted your spiritual growth. Write down any changes you have noticed in your life or character as a result of worship and how you can continue to seek transformation through it.

Aligning Your Thoughts

Date

YOU WERE NOT CREATED BY ACCIDENT, BUT DESIGNED
WITH DIVINE PRECISION FOR A PURPOSE ONLY YOU CAN FULFILL.

OBEDIENCE
IS THE
PATHWAY FORWARD

THIS IS PLUMB

One surrendered step at a time is still purpose in motion.

THIS IS NOT

I have to have it all figured out.

"Your word is a lamp to my feet and a light to my path." –
Psalm 119:105

CLOSING JOURNAL:

THE POWER OF WORSHIP IN DAILY LIFE

1. REFLECTION ON WORSHIP THIS WEEK

How did I incorporate worship into my daily life this week? Were there moments where worship (through music, prayer, or action) shifted my focus or perspective? In what ways did I feel God's presence during times of worship?

2. WORSHIP AS A LIFESTYLE

How did I express worship beyond the traditional setting (e.g., at work, with family, in my personal thoughts)? How has worship impacted my attitude, decisions, or interactions with others this week?
What does it mean for me to live a life of worship in every moment?

3. THE POWER OF WORSHIP

How did worship empower me this week?
Were there specific challenges or struggles that worship helped me overcome?
How did worship strengthen my faith or bring peace to difficult situations?

4. GRATITUDE AND ACKNOWLEDGMENT

List three ways God has revealed Himself this week through worship. How has worship deepened my understanding of God's character and love for me?

CLOSING JOURNAL:

5. PRAYER OF SURRENDER AND PRAISE

Write a prayer of surrender, thanking God for the power of worship in your life, and asking for continued guidance in making worship a daily habit.

6. LOOKING AHEAD

How can I make worship a more intentional part of my life in the coming week? What practical ways can I glorify God in everyday moments?

Aligning Your Thoughts

Date ____________________

YOU WERE NOT CREATED BY ACCIDENT, BUT DESIGNED
WITH DIVINE PRECISION FOR A PURPOSE ONLY YOU CAN FULFILL.

FOLLOW-UP

GROWTH ASSESSMENT

Time has passed, as you've continued your journey through this devotional.

Now, take a moment to reassess your spiritual growth. Reflect on how you have changed since the last assessment. Have you deepened your roots, grown stronger in faith, or overcome areas of spiritual dryness? Refer to the instructions at the beginning of the devotional (page 8) if you need a refresher.

Using the blank plant image again, update your reflection:

Roots: Have they grown deeper in faith?
What has strengthened or weakened your foundation?

Leaves: Are you bearing new spiritual fruit? What has improved, and where do you still see struggles?

Watering Can: What are you feeding your spirit now? Have you cultivated healthy spiritual nourishment, or are there areas still in need of refreshment?

Reflection Questions for Follow-Up:

How have I grown spiritually since my first assessment?
What new spiritual habits or disciplines have I developed?
Where do I still feel challenged in my spiritual walk?
What fruit of the Spirit has become more evident in my life?
What steps can I take moving forward to continue thriving?
No matter your progress, remember: God is always at work in you. Every step taken in faith leads to greater growth. Keep tending your soul, staying rooted in Him, and trusting that He is shaping you for His purpose.

WHERE I AM

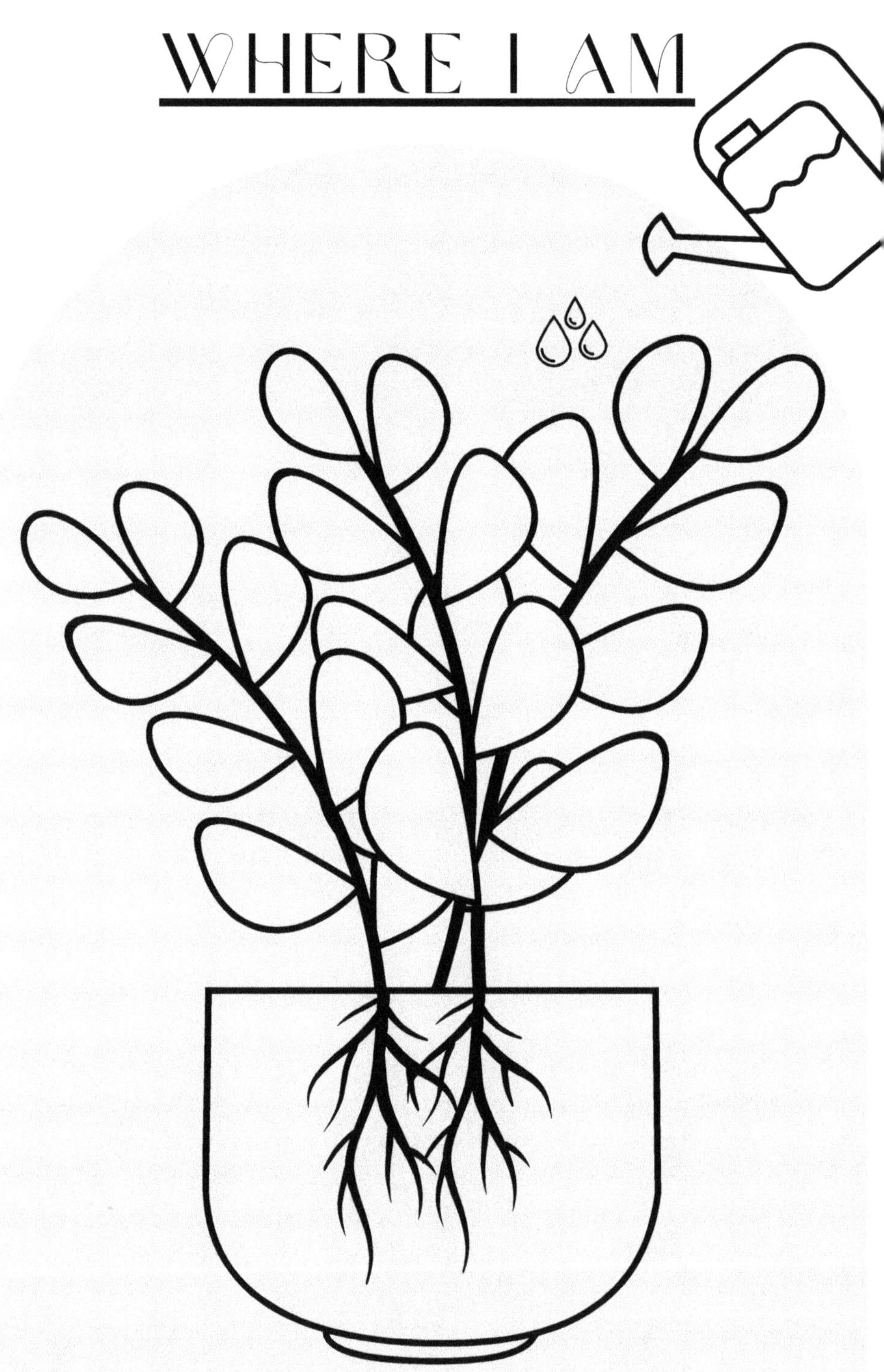

BONUS
SECTION

DISCOVERING YOUR SPIRITUAL GIFTS

Recognizing the Gifts God Has Placed Within You
"Each of you should use whatever gift you have received to serve others,
as faithful stewards of God's grace…"
 —1 Peter 4:10 (NIV)

Purpose:
God has uniquely equipped every believer with spiritual gifts—divine abilities that empower us to serve, encourage, and build up others in the body of Christ. These gifts are not earned; they are given through the Holy Spirit. Understanding your spiritual gifts helps you walk more confidently in your purpose and find joy in serving others.

Some common gifts include:
- Teaching – Making spiritual truth understandable
- Wisdom – Applying deep understanding to life and others
- Leadership – Guiding others with vision and care
- Prophecy – Speaking God's truth boldly and timely
- Encouragement (Exhortation) – Uplifting and motivating others
- Discernment – Recognizing truth, error, or spiritual dynamics
- Faith – Trusting God deeply and inspiring faith in others
- Mercy – Showing compassion with ease
- Giving – Joyfully meeting needs with generosity
- Hospitality – Creating a welcoming, warm environment
- Administration – Organizing and bringing order to tasks or teams
- Evangelism – Sharing the gospel with clarity and boldness
- Healing – Being used by God to bring restoration

SPIRITUAL GIFT ASSESSMENT

Instructions: Use a scale of 1–5 to rate how true each statement is of you. (1 = Not at all | 3 = Sometimes | 5 = Very true)

	1-5
I enjoy organizing details and making things efficient.	
People often come to me for advice or spiritual direction.	
I feel compelled to encourage others when they're discouraged.	
I enjoy explaining biblical truths to others.	
I can sense when something feels off spiritually.	
I find joy in giving generously to people or ministries.	
I often trust God easily, even in hard seasons.	
I love creating a welcoming, peaceful environment for others.	
I'm deeply moved by other people's pain.	
I often feel a burden to pray for others—even strangers.	
I like guiding groups or taking initiative in decision-making.	
I believe God can heal and often pray in faith for that.	
I enjoy helping behind the scenes and don't need recognition.	
I feel called to stand against injustice and speak truth.	
I often experience dreams, insights, or messages that feel spiritual.	
I enjoy sharing the gospel and helping others know Jesus.	
I often imagine creative ways to meet people's needs.	
I feel renewed when I make space for beauty, rest, or God's presence.	

Circle the statements you rated 4 or 5, then look for recurring themes. Your highest-rated areas reveal your strongest spiritual gifts.

MATCHING YOUR SCORES TO GIFT CATEGORIES

If you scored high on...	You may have the gift of...
ADMINISTRATION	Organizing, planning structure
WISDOM	Creativity and solution-oriented thinking; giving advice or direction
EXHORTATION: (Encouragement)	Encouraging others, uplifting hearts
TEACHING	Explaining and clarifying the word of God
DISCERNMENT	Sensing things spiritually
GIVING	Generosity
FAITH	Trusting God easily
HOSPITALITY	Hosting or welcoming others; creating space for peace and worship
MERCY	Feeling others' emotions deeply
INTERCESSION	Passionate prayer life, praying for healing
LEADERSHIP	Taking initiative or leading others
HEALING	Praying for healing
SERVING / HELPS	Working behind the scenes; action, support, insight
PROPHECY	Hearing God through dreams or impressions; receiving spiritual insight
EVANGELISM	Sharing Jesus with others

REFLECTION QUESTIONS

WHICH 3–5 STATEMENTS DID YOU SCORE HIGHEST?

____
____
____

WHAT PATTERNS DO YOU NOTICE?

____
____
____

HAVE OTHERS AFFIRMED THESE QUALITIES IN YOU?

____
____
____

HOW DO THESE GIFTS MAKE YOU FEEL WHEN YOU'RE
USING THEM?

____
____
____

CLOSING ENCOURAGEMENT
"We have different gifts, according to the grace given to each of
us…"
—Romans 12:6

Dear sister, God has gifted you uniquely. You don't have to "do it all."
Just be faithful with what He's entrusted to you. Trust that as you
grow in intimacy with Him, He'll make your purpose clearer and
your impact deeper.

THE PROCESS OF PLUMB LINING GOD'S TRUTH IN OUR LIVES

1. Seek Understanding

Pray for Insight: Begin with prayer, asking God to reveal His truth to you. Seek a deeper understanding of God's Word and how it applies to your life.

Read Scripture: Make it a habit to engage with the Bible daily. Focus on passages that speak to your current circumstances, challenges, and questions.

2. Identify Core Truths

Reflect on God's Promises: As you read, jot down the truths and promises you find in Scripture.

Create Affirmations: Turn these truths into positive affirmations. Declare them over your life regularly, allowing them to shape your mindset.

3. Self-Examination

Assess Your Beliefs: Reflect on your thoughts, beliefs, and attitudes. Are they aligned with God's truth? Identify any lies or negative beliefs that may be influencing you.

Journal Your Insights: Use a journal to document your reflections and insights as you explore the truths
of Scripture, allowing this to deepen your understanding.

4. Align Your Actions

Take Practical Steps: Consider how you can implement God's truth into your daily life. This may involve making intentional decisions or changing habits that are inconsistent with His Word.

Seek Accountability: Share your journey with a trusted friend or mentor who can encourage you and
help you stay accountable to the changes you're making.

By actively engaging in this process, you will cultivate a life rooted in God's truth, allowing it to guide and transform you in every aspect of life.

THE PROCESS OF PLUMB LINING GOD'S TRUTH IN OUR LIVES

5. WORSHIP & PRAISE

Engage in Worship: Use worship as a powerful tool to reinforce God's truths in your life. Singing, praying, and meditating on His goodness will help shift your focus and strengthen your faith.
Celebrate His Faithfulness: Take time to acknowledge and celebrate the ways you've seen God's truth
at work in your life.

6. EMBRACE TRANSFORMATION

Allow Change: Be open to how God is transforming your heart, mind, and actions. Trust that aligning
with His truth is a process of growth.
Reflect on Progress: Periodically reflect on how your understanding and application of God's truth
has evolved over time.

7. SHARE THE TRUTH

Encourage Others: Share your experiences and insights with others. Discussing God's truth can uplift and encourage those around you.
Live as a Witness: Let your life be a testimony of God's truth. Your words and actions should reflect His love and grace to those you encounter.

By actively engaging in this process, you will cultivate a life rooted in God's truth, allowing it to guide and transform you in every aspect of life.

As you've journeyed through each theme in this devotional, you've been invited to realign with God's truth — not just in part, but in every area of your life. This process of plumb lining is not about perfection; it's about positioning — choosing to live measured, surrendered, and anchored in Him. My prayer is that these 48 days awaken a lifelong pursuit of wholeness, and that you now move forward with clarity, confidence, and the courage to live plumbed for purpose.

ABOUT THE AUTHOR

Michel Hernandez is a pursuer of Christ, wife, mother, intercessor, and mentor. For the past 18 years, she and her husband have built a life together, raising a beautifully blended family of five daughters—three of whom she birthed, and all of whom she loves deeply. Like many blended families, their journey has included both closeness and distance, moments of deep connection and seasons of challenge. Through it all, Michel's prayers have covered each daughter, trusting God to complete His work in their lives.

Michel's relationship with Jesus began on Mother's Day in 2005, when she surrendered her life to Him and was baptized in the Spirit. Since then, her faith has been refined through seasons of joy, loss, waiting, and perseverance. In May 2024, shortly after moving to Oklahoma, Michel sensed God leading her to set aside her own plans and trust His timing. In that place of surrender, the vision for Plumbed for Purpose began to take root.

To Michel, being "plumbed" means walking closely with Jesus and aligning every part of life with His truth—resisting the pull of distraction, busyness, and worldly measures of success. It's about intimacy with Him above all else. When she's not pouring into her family, Michel faithfully stands alongside her husband, praying for and supporting his work as he mentors and counsels men in their community. She finds her deepest connection with God in the secret place of prayer and in the moments of struggle where His presence meets her most powerfully.

Her prayer is that every woman who turns these pages will walk away with renewed peace, clarity, and a closer relationship with Jesus—meeting Him face to face.

PLUMBED FOR PURPOSE: THE TRUTH

Being plumbed for purpose isn't about chasing a title, platform, or destination that looks like someone else's—it's about **alignment with God through relationship**. In a culture that elevates self and rewards performance, we're called to a different standard.

When we are plumbed, we live upright in a crooked generation.

We don't bend to trends—we anchor to truth.

We don't hustle for worth—we rest in identity.

We don't perform to be seen—we live to reflect His glory.

To be plumbed is to live worshipfully—rooted in God's Word, led by the Holy Spirit, and aligned with truth, even when it's uncomfortable. This kind of purpose is not measured by accolades, but by how deeply our lives reflect the character of Christ.

Your purpose is not a destination. It's a direction.

It's a way of being, shaped by intimacy with Jesus.

And ultimately, it's about one thing—glorifying God with your whole life.

-MICHEL HERNANDEZ